RECEIVING THE WISDOM OF GOD

Retreat Leader Guide
WORKBOOK
RICHARD T. CASE

To my wife, Linda, who is a true partner in seeking God's wisdom together. She has a wonderful heart to hear, and to fully participate in the process of receiving God's wisdom for our life "stuff" that is personal and real to us. She knows and continues to remind me that we fundamentally do not know or have real wisdom since we are limited in understanding and do not know what is "around the corner—what is ahead in the future" that God knows. So, she encourages us to always seek God's wisdom—since such a privilege, why wouldn't we? Her insights and ideas that she brings to the process is truly such a joy to experience as we receive together God's truth and wisdom for us. I am blessed to have such a partner that stands together in this privilege—best and none better.

Acknowledgments

We wish to thank all of the leaders of our **Ministry: Living Waters—ABIDE Ministries!** These leaders fully understand seeking God's wisdom and live in this wisdom all the time. They personally assist us in confirming God's wisdom for us and for the ministry. These leaders are wonderful examples of how to seek, receive and follow God's wisdom, so that all those that come to retreats and the ones they are discipling are learning how valuable this is to be living out life on a real, practical level. Thank you all for being such true followers of Christ and His Wisdom.

These leaders are:

Jake & Mary Beckel
Joe & Leigh Bogar
Rich & Janet Cocchiaro
Larry & Sherry Collet
Scott & Kristen Cornell
David & Melissa Dunkel
Tom & Susanne Ewing
Rick & Kelly Ferris
Joel & Christina Gunn
Scott & Terry Hitchcock
Chris & Jaclyn Hoover
Rick & Nancy Hoover
Tad & Monica Jones
Ed & Becky Kobel
Don & Rachelle Light
Chris & Heidi May
Terry & Josephine Noetzel
Steve & Carolyn Van Ooteghem
Preston & Lynda Pitts
Dan & Kathy Rocconi
Bob & Keri Rockwell
John & Michelle Santaferraro
Allyson & Denny Weinberg
Neal & Kathy Weisenburger

RECEIVING THE WISDOM OF GOD
PUBLISHED BY LIVING WATERS—ABIDE MINISTRIES
7615 Lemon Gulch Way
Castle Rock, CO 80108

Unless otherwise noted, all Scripture quotations are from the ESV® Bible (The Holy Bible, English Standard Version®), copyright © 2001 by Crossway Bibles, a publishing ministry of Good News Publishers. Used by permission. All rights reserved.

ISBN: 978-1-7379372-1-0
Copyright © 2024 by Richard T. Case.

All rights reserved. No part of this publication may be reproduced, distributed or transmitted in any form or by any means, including photocopying, recording, or other electronic or mechanical methods, without the prior written permission of the publisher.

Publisher's Cataloging-in-Publication data

Names:
Title:
Description: .
Identifiers: ISBN | LCCN
Subjects:

Printed in the United States of America 2024 — 1st ed

TABLE OF CONTENTS

Introduction: 2

Lesson One:
What is Wisdom?. 4

Lesson Two:
Deeper Level of Wisdom/Our Benefits 20

Lesson Three:
How Do We Receive This Wisdom 40

Lesson Four:
Experiencing the Fullness of Wisdom—The Supernatural 60

INTRODUCTION

What is your definition of "Wisdom"? and "The Supernatural"? Write the unresolved issues in your life and the questions/decisions you are facing for the uncertain times ahead. Where do you seek wisdom and God's supernatural work to bring clarity and resolution right now?

_____
_____
_____
_____
_____
_____
_____
_____
_____
_____
_____
_____
_____
_____
_____
_____
_____
_____
_____
_____

INTRODUCTION

LESSON 1:
WHAT IS WISDOM?

1. **What is "wisdom?"**

How do these verses define wisdom? What does that mean personally?

> **Read Proverbs 1:1-7:**
>
> The Beginning of Knowledge
> ¹ The proverbs of Solomon, son of David, king of Israel:
> ² To know wisdom and instruction,
>   to understand words of insight,
> ³ to receive instruction in wise dealing,
>   in righteousness, justice, and equity;
> ⁴ to give prudence to the simple,
>   knowledge and discretion to the youth—
> ⁵ Let the wise hear and increase in learning,
>   and the one who understands obtain guidance,
> ⁶ to understand a proverb and a saying,
>   the words of the wise and their riddles.
> ⁷ The fear of the Lord is the beginning of knowledge;
>   fools despise wisdom and instruction.

"Our role is to receive the guidance. If we're hearing it, if we're receiving it, by definition, it's because God is always giving it."

_____
_____
_____
_____
_____
_____

What is wisdom? Understanding, justice, judgment, equity, discretion; we will be taught which way to walk, will understand it clearly, and have discernment along the way. What does it mean? We'll have direction and guidance on which way to go. This is all applied to each of us personally. It's not broad philosophy. These are all very specific words. If

LESSON 1:
WHAT IS WISDOM?

we want instruction, what do we want instruction for? What's going on in our life? We'll have instruction, we'll have understanding, we'll have counsel, and we'll have guidance for the decisions, the activities, the issues, the problems in our lives as they apply to us.

    Our role is to receive the guidance. If we're hearing it, if we're receiving it, by definition, it's because God is always giving it. It's not really that complicated. Are we figuring it out? Are we using our great logic to analyze things and say, "I can come up with my own answer?" No. Wisdom comes when God gives us instruction, counsel, and guidance. We are to put ourselves in a receiving mode.

We must understand how to receive this.

Word Definitions:

wisdom: skill (in war), managing, administration, shrewdness, prudence – to be made wise

instruction: being taught, directed, corrected, chastened

words: utterance, speech, saying, promise, command

understanding: discernment

receive: to take, get, fetch, lay hold of, seize

hear: listen, give heed, to consent, agree

learning: being taught, gaining insight

attain: to get, acquire, create, buy, possess

counsels: direction, guidance, good advice

What does this mean to hate evil, pride, and arrogance? How do we follow this in our everyday lives?

Read Proverbs 8:12-14:

[12] "I, wisdom, dwell with prudence,
    and I find knowledge and discretion.
[13] The fear of the Lord is hatred of evil.
Pride and arrogance and the way of evil
    and perverted speech I hate.
[14] I have counsel and sound wisdom;
    I have insight; I have strength.

LESSON 1:
WHAT IS WISDOM?

_____
_____
_____
_____
_____

As we begin to pursue wisdom, He says one of the truths is to hate evil. Now, the word here isn't dark or awful, which in our normal understanding is to simply agree that we hate evil. The Hebrew word is annoyance, harassment, difficulty, pain, stress, affliction, oppression. He's saying the things in life that cause us to be annoyed, oppressed, difficult, things that are coming against us or aren't working well—all of which He's labeled as evil.

And remember, it's just that simple. Why is it evil? Because it is not of God. And He says to hate it. Hate these annoying things that are happening to us or are against us. We don't need to put up with this because they're not of God. So, He says the beginning of wisdom comes when we say we don't need to live with this. He said, if we're going to receive wisdom, we should start by saying and realizing that we are experiencing this difficulty, which isn't of God and thus God has an answer for this (i.e., wisdom).

Does it mean we'll never experience difficulty? No, because "in the world you'll have trouble." Jesus says, "I've overcome it." (We, by the way, have an entire course called "Overcoming Adversity, which teaches the depth of overcoming.) The premise of this simply is that we don't have to put up with it. Wisdom says, don't put up with it. And so, a lot of people, because they believe that everything happens for some reason, believe that everything is God's will. "We're experiencing this annoying thing in our life, which is constantly frustrating to us, so it must be God's will." If we believe everything is God's will and it constantly is annoying us, our attitude is going to be what? Well, that must be God's will.

He stops us there, reminding us that if we actually understand wisdom, we should know to hate the annoyance and say, "We don't need to put up with this; absolutely not." Through the revelation of God's wisdom, we will start to receive answers about this.

Further, we should hate pride and arrogance. Who is He talking about? Each of us. Pride and arrogance come when we think we know better and are stubborn about it. We just keep doing what we are doing because we think we know better. He says: "If you're going to have wisdom, you really have to get these two points settled. You don't need to put up with this ridiculous stuff that's happening to you; and don't think you know better than Me. I can give you answers and lead you to the best; to resolve your issues and not have you live any longer in the frustration that is not of Me."

LESSON 1:
WHAT IS WISDOM?

Word Definitions:

dwell: abide, reside

prudence: craftiness, shrewdness

knowledge: perception, skill, discernment, understanding

inventions: plans, purposes, creative thoughts

fear: respect, reverence, awe

evil: full of labors, annoyances, hardships; pressed and harassed by labors; bringing toils, annoyances, perils; of a time full of peril to Christian faith and steadfastness; causing pain and trouble; bad, of a bad nature or condition; in a

physical sense: diseased or blind

pride: lifting, exalting oneself up

arrogant: stubborn, unwilling to listen or learn

strength: might

How does this define the fear of the Lord? What does that mean personally? Why is this so important in receiving wisdom?

> **Read Proverbs 9:10-12:**
>
> [10] The fear of the Lord is the beginning of wisdom,
>   and the knowledge of the Holy One is insight.
> [11] For by me your days will be multiplied,
>   and years will be added to your life.
> [12] If you are wise, you are wise for yourself;
>   if you scoff, you alone will bear it.

_____
_____
_____
_____
_____

LESSON 1:
WHAT IS WISDOM?

The fear of the Lord is the beginning of wisdom. What is the fear of the Lord? The knowledge that He's all knowing and has all the answers, has all the wisdom about everything and knows the best way for us to walk.

There's no other better way. We must surrender our own intellect, our will, to what He would have to say. Fear means that we are in awe of, or follow something, because of that awe. To whom do we surrender? We're either in awe of Him or instead are in awe of the world, or in awe of sophistication or logic or the world's approach.

In other words, what do we put our trust in? He says, "The beginning of true wisdom is to put your faith, your trust, your heart in God." This means we believe what He's going to tell us is absolutely true, even when we don't completely understand it. That is why it's hard for us. We don't get it or we don't understand it, so we may as well go a different way.

He says, "In all cases, the fear of the Lord is the beginning of wisdom. Seek Me first and always, and I will show you the way—first and always. What My Bible says is true—always. So, when you do not understand it, or when it seems to be contradictory, know it is true and continue to seek Me. I will show you the truth, the answers."

Word Definition: **fear:** respect, reverence – looks to Him and knows that what He says is true

What do these verses in Exodus and Daniel tell us about wisdom? What does this mean to us in our walk of life? Why?

> **Read Exodus 35:30–36:2:**
>
> Construction of the Tabernacle
> [30] Then Moses said to the people of Israel, "See, the Lord has called by name Bezalel the son of Uri, son of Hur, of the tribe of Judah; [31] and he has filled him with the Spirit of God, with skill, with intelligence, with knowledge, and with all craftsmanship, [32] to devise artistic designs, to work in gold and silver and bronze, [33] in cutting stones for setting, and in carving wood, for work in every skilled craft. [34] And he has inspired him to teach, both him and Oholiab the son of Ahisamach of the tribe of Dan. [35] He has filled them with skill to do every sort of work done by an engraver or by a designer or by an embroiderer in blue and purple and scarlet yarns and fine twined linen, or by a weaver—by any sort of workman or skilled designer.

LESSON 1:
WHAT IS WISDOM?

> ³⁶ "Bezalel and Oholiab and every craftsman in whom the Lord has put skill and intelligence to know how to do any work in the construction of the sanctuary shall work in accordance with all that the Lord has commanded."
>
> ² And Moses called Bezalel and Oholiab and every craftsman in whose mind the Lord had put skill, everyone whose heart stirred him up to come to do the work.

_____

_____

_____

_____

Word Definitions:

filled: overflowing, full, abundant

workmanship: occupation, business

devise: to think, plan, esteem, calculate, invent, make a judgment, imagine, count

works: invented plans

heart: soul, inner man

work: to do, accomplish, fashion, produce

put: to give, bestow, grant, permit, ascribe, employ, devote, consecrate, dedicate, pay wages, sell, exchange, lend, commit, entrust, give over, deliver

do: same as work; accomplish, fashion, produce

> **Read Daniel 1:4, 17, 20:**
>
> ⁴ youths without blemish, of good appearance and skillful in all wisdom, endowed with knowledge, understanding learning, and competent to stand in the king's palace, and to teach them the literature and language of the Chaldeans.
>
> ¹⁷ As for these four youths, God gave them learning and skill in all literature and wisdom, and Daniel had understanding in all visions and dreams.
>
> ²⁰ And in every matter of wisdom and understanding about which the king inquired of them, he found them ten times better than all the magicians and enchanters that were in all his kingdom.

LESSON 1:
WHAT IS WISDOM?

_____
_____
_____
_____
_____

Wisdom includes our skills and the activities to which we are to engage our skills. We tend to think of wisdom as having the right decisions. But God tells us it's much larger than that. Wisdom will translate into creativity, into insight, and into understanding as we apply ourselves to the work that He's calling us to whether we are housewives, mothers, homebuilders, accountants, or musicians. He will give us the wisdom to apply our skill in a creative way to do that work. He's going to give us the creativity and skill to apply it to fulfilling all that He's calling us to do. It will be born of the Spirit and will spill forth with excellence.

Consider Daniel and his friends. They were captured. They had lived in Israel, in a society that they were used to, but then they were captured and put into a foreign location. They were placed in a completely "non-Jewish" place (an atheistic, non-Godly place), and they had to be educated in a brand new system. What did God give them? Wisdom, which was the ability to learn the new system really, really well. Actually, it was so well that Nebuchadnezzar said that they were 10 times better than those he had had for years. They learned quickly and were even given a supernatural ability to interpret dreams (the spiritual element of discernment).

While we're learning in the area of our profession or our work assignment at the moment, or whatever practical thing we're involved in, He says, "I'll show you how to be skilled in this area and will offer the wisdom for the application that you need. You will be effective at this. In every case, it will be the best. It's not half-hearted. It's not just a little bit. It's everything you need to know to fulfill what I've called you to be part of in an excellent way."

It's going to be instruction, understanding, guidance, and what He wants to do—the giving of skill and the application of that skill in creative and understanding ways to produce excellence.

Word Definitions:

favored: vision (supernatural), well favored, sight, vision (power of seeing)
learning: book learning – understanding
visions: prophetic oracle
dreams: prophetic meaning
matters: business, occupation, acts, case

LESSON 1:
WHAT IS WISDOM?

Write in journal: What elements of wisdom are particularly important to you right now? Why?

2. What is "wisdom" really?

What is the difference between worldly wisdom and God's wisdom? How will we know the difference in our lives? Why is this important for us in our everyday lives?

> **Read James 3:13-18:**
>
> Wisdom from Above
> [13] Who is wise and understanding among you? By his good conduct let him show his works in the meekness of wisdom. [14] But if you have bitter jealousy and selfish ambition in your hearts, do not boast and be false to the truth. [15] This is not the wisdom that comes down from above, but is earthly, unspiritual, demonic. [16] For where jealousy and selfish ambition exist, there will be disorder and every vile practice. [17] But the wisdom from above is first pure, then peaceable, gentle, open to reason, full of mercy and good fruits, impartial and sincere. [18] And a harvest of righteousness is sown in peace by those who make peace.

_____
_____
_____
_____

Earthly wisdom, worldly wisdom, and wisdom from the enemy are characterized as: jealousy, ambition, boasting, and disorder, all of which are ultimately confusing. As we are seeking wisdom, one tendency is to seek input from others, even Christian friends. Usually this brings about more confusion, as we receive all these different opinions. This worldly wisdom is based on their own earthly experience. It's actually coming from, in a sense, a demonic place, a sensual, human place. And thus, it's confusing.

LESSON 1:
WHAT IS WISDOM?

Then, we are more confused than ever because it's coming from the world, so we are left to our self-centered analysis to try to figure things out. This is pride. What's it based on? The fact that we think we should do something a certain way… and with limited information. Even though we don't know everything about it with the limited information we've been given, we still try to figure it out, based upon our own view of it – even though we are confused. So, we are receiving worldly, demonic wisdom, and staying in this wisdom by trying to figure it out on our own. It is not going to work out well.

But if we see God's wisdom is from above, what are the qualities of God's wisdom?

Pure, peaceable, gentle: It's a spiritual thing. It starts to resonate with what the Spirit is telling us. And we come to the same place of shalom. We receive confirmation in our Sprit because there is purity about that. There's a clarity about that. It's good, there's an excellence about that. It's leading us to the best. He's trying to say, "Stay with Me until you get confirmation, because if it's from Me, it will come together, and you can confidently say: 'I see it now. It's from Him.'" And we can confirm it's from Him because it's the shalom of the Spirit and it'll be without confusion. It won't be ambiguous.

Word Definitions:

earthly: worldly
sensual: selfish appetites and passions
confusion: disorder, disturbance
pure: exciting reverence; full of God's goodness
peaceable: bringing God's favor and best
gentle: equitable, fair, mild
intreated: compliant
mercy: good will; heart for disadvantaged
good: pleasant, agreeable (to the senses); pleasant (to the higher nature), excellent, rich, valuable in estimation
glad: happy, prosperous
partiality: without ambiguity or uncertainty
hypocrisy: playing a part, acting without believing

What wisdom did God give Daniel? On what basis did God give it? What does that mean for us and how do we receive it?

LESSON 1:
WHAT IS WISDOM?

Read Daniel 2:20-23; 29-30:

[20] Daniel answered and said:
"Blessed be the name of God forever and ever,
  to whom belong wisdom and might.
[21] He changes times and seasons;
  he removes kings and sets up kings;
he gives wisdom to the wise
  and knowledge to those who have understanding;
[22] he reveals deep and hidden things;
  he knows what is in the darkness,
  and the light dwells with him.
[23] To you, O God of my fathers,
  I give thanks and praise,
for you have given me wisdom and might,
  and have now made known to me what we asked of you,
  for you have made known to us the king's matter."

[29] To you, O king, as you lay in bed came thoughts of what would be after this, and he who reveals mysteries made known to you what is to be. [30] But as for me, this mystery has been revealed to me, not because of any wisdom that I have more than all the living, but in order that the interpretation may be made known to the king, and that you may know the thoughts of your mind.

_____
_____
_____
_____
_____

    God gave to Daniel secrets, hidden things, revelations, power, might, things that weren't known normally. God will make known those hidden things and will make known those things that nobody else can know. And now who makes it known to Daniel? God. And Daniel understood something about this—that it had nothing to do with him. Why is that good news?

LESSON 1:
WHAT IS WISDOM?

Because that means it is not only special people who receive it. He reveals it to all His children who have a heart to receive it—meaning us, too. We tend to think that Daniel was really smart. Instead, Daniel says, "I didn't receive any of this based on anything that has to do with me. Therefore, you can receive it, too." Others are not more spiritual than we are, or more skilled than we are, or more mature than we are.

Daniel clearly understood this. He was not receiving wisdom because of anything that had to do with him. It was all because it comes from God and thus all God's children can receive it. No one is exempt or restricted from receiving it.

God will reveal secret information to all who have a heart to receive—all, meaning all of us. Why is this such good news?

Word Definitions:
might: power, strength
gives: provides
reveals: uncover, disclose
secret: hidden, unknown to us naturally
made known: caused to be informed

What do these verses say about wisdom? Who really is wisdom, and why then is this important to us personally?

Read 1 Corinthians 1:21-30:

[21] For since, in the wisdom of God, the world did not know God through wisdom, it pleased God through the folly of what we preach[a] to save those who believe. [22] For Jews demand signs and Greeks seek wisdom, [23] but we preach Christ crucified, a stumbling block to Jews and folly to Gentiles, [24] but to those who are called, both Jews and Greeks, Christ the power of God and the wisdom of God. [25] For the foolishness of God is wiser than men, and the weakness of God is stronger than men.

[26] For consider your calling, brothers: not many of you were wise according to worldly standards,[b] not many were powerful, not many were of noble birth. [27] But God chose what is foolish in the world to shame the wise; God chose what is weak in the world to shame the strong; [28] God chose what is low and despised in the world, even things that are not, to bring to nothing things that are, [29] so that no human being[c] might boast in the presence of God. [30] And because of him[d] you are in Christ Jesus, who became to us wisdom from God, righteousness and sanctification and redemption,

LESSON 1:
WHAT IS WISDOM?

_____
_____
_____
_____
_____

He says: We are not to look in any way to what the world considers to be wisdom. Why? Who is wisdom? Christ. Christ in us is all the wisdom we'll ever need. Wisdom is already there—in anyone who is a believer.

It's not an amorphous thing, it's not out in space somewhere. It's not philosophical or something we have to qualify for with intellect or ability or spiritual maturity or conditions.

It's because it is Christ Himself. It's His wisdom that will make its way into our everyday lives. We will have the ability to hear it because it's in us. And it doesn't take sophistication because it's not a system. If it were a system and there was sophistication to it, then we'd have to be taught that system. We'd have to learn it and if we don't, we can use that as an excuse. This is like mathematics, or geometry, or something else that we aren't good at. And then we could say: "I couldn't learn it so it justifies why I can't get it." It's not that at all: It's a person in relationship — in us. And He'll translate it so we can hear it uniquely. He gives it to us because it's a relationship. That's how beautiful this is, because the wisdom is Him.

Word Definitions: **sign:** unusual occurrence
wisdom: the thoughts and understanding of mankind (science)
stumbling block: snare, trap
foolishness: does not make sense
power: splendor, majesty, beauty, vigor, glory, in-charge, control, have jurisdiction, power to influence, cause to become great; much; many; enlarged, exceedingly abundant, power (physical and spiritual) of doing supernatural, right to govern, rule, command - possessing authority, mighty work, strength, miracle, performing miracles, excellence

LESSON 1:
WHAT IS WISDOM?

righteousness: integrity, virtue, purity of life, rightness, correctness of thinking, feeling, and acting

sanctification: transformation of heart and life

redemption: deliverance, being made whole

Knowing that Christ is wisdom and that He gives wisdom to us, what do these verses tell us that are important to our lives? Why?

> **Read Colossians 2:1-3; 9-10:**
>
> **2** For I want you to know how great a struggle I have for you and for those at Laodicea and for all who have not seen me face to face, ² that their hearts may be encouraged, being knit together in love, to reach all the riches of full assurance of understanding and the knowledge of God's mystery, which is Christ, ³ in whom are hidden all the treasures of wisdom and knowledge.
>
> ⁹ For in him the whole fullness of deity dwells bodily, ¹⁰ and you have been filled in him, who is the head of all rule and authority.

_____
_____
_____
_____
_____

    All the fullness, all the treasures, which are secrets that He'll give us, are all in Him, complete in Him. All the treasures of wisdom are complete in Him. And we are complete in Him. The fullness of wisdom resides in us completely. Is there anything missing at this very moment? No. But there is a tension. Are we perfect? No. We must not then associate wisdom with perfection.

    We say, "Aren't we going to be being transformed the rest of our life?" Yes. He will be transforming the rest of our lives, but do we have all the wisdom? Yes. So, are we walking through life needing wisdom? Yes, since we need this every minute, every day, He says the fullness of that is already in us, and since we are not perfect, we are needing to be transformed during our life. This is ongoing and everlasting. We will constantly need wisdom for how to live, including:

LESSON 1:
WHAT IS WISDOM?

1. Healing of a wound that needs transformation.

2. Making a decision. Knowing what to do.

3. Solving a problem. Determining how to do it.

It's all practical and it's unique to who we all are. That's why we don't have a right to judge. The people next to us are living a different course of wisdom, a different course of life, and they must receive their wisdom of God for their path—not from us but from God.

So, fullness means what? Everything and always, at all times—unique to our life—all is available to us while we walk through life being transformed. It's not a requirement of being perfect. We have all the fullness, all the answers and everything in us to live out the life, the path, that God has ordained for us. We can be imperfect and struggling while receiving the fullness of the wisdom that is needed for the current path. Nothing will be missing. All we are to do is to receive what is already there and to be received at the moment. It never ends, so there is more to receive; we shall have the fullness but not all at once and not have to be perfect to receive the fullness that is in us now. This is an amazing truth that is profound and beautiful. Why are we to live in joy and peace all the time, even as we live in a world of trouble? He says we have all the fullness of Him in us, and nothing will be withheld as we walk with Him. Not that we are or need to be perfect, but rather to enjoy life in this fullness.

Word Definitions: **treasure:** the place in which good and precious things are collected and laid up; a coffin where valuables are kept
filled: with the presence, power, agency, riches of God and of Christ
complete: caused to be filled to the full, abundantly, abounding

What do these verses say about the Spirit of wisdom? What is the difference between spiritual wisdom and worldly (natural) wisdom? Why is this so important for us in our lives?

> **Read Isaiah 11:1-3:**
>
> The Righteous Reign of the Branch
> **11** There shall come forth a shoot from the stump of Jesse,
>   and a branch from his roots shall bear fruit.

LESSON 1:
WHAT IS WISDOM?

> ² And the Spirit of the Lord shall rest upon him,
>   the Spirit of wisdom and understanding,
>   the Spirit of counsel and might,
>   the Spirit of knowledge and the fear of the Lord.
> ³ And his delight shall be in the fear of the Lord.
> He shall not judge by what his eyes see,
>   or decide disputes by what his ears hear,

_____
_____
_____
_____
_____

Wisdom, which is in Christ, which is also in us, is a spiritual process. We are thus not to function according to the natural, that which we see and process; rather we are to get wisdom and understanding, counsel and knowledge from Him. Our clarity is promised because it's a spiritual process which we have privilege to because He's in us, residing in each of us. We no longer have to figure this out by what we observe in our own logic trying to determine whether something is natural or worldly.

He doesn't say throw out our ability to reason with Him and process things, but He says rely on it because it's spiritual. He's going to tell us secrets. He's going to tell us wisdom. He's going to tell us things that we cannot receive naturally but only things that He knows and must reveal to us. It's all available to us. And it's the Spirit of Christ, which resides in us. So therefore, it's a spiritual process.

For example: Joshua was willing to follow God into the promised land and went to battle in the city of Jericho. How did they win Jericho? They marched around the city, blew their trumpets, and the walls fell in. Joshua could have said, "Hey, that's a great technique. I like that technique. Let's go do that again, let's go use that to win battles. Doesn't that make sense? What a great way to win a battle. Let's go march around the cities and blow the trumpets to win all our battles that way." Interestingly enough, they never do that again.

Because God is unique in applying wisdom to everything, we must be careful. We can't just go marching around the city and claim the city because we believe we should. Haven't we forgotten something? We need to remember to always ask God.

LESSON 1:
WHAT IS WISDOM?

One thing is for sure. Wisdom is not received naturally from the world or from our own logic. It's a spirit that is in us; it's Christ, and He will give it to us.

Word Definitions: **wisdom:** understanding, counsel, might
knowledge: perception, skill, discernment, understanding
sight: what is seen naturally
hearing: what other people say, rumor

Write in journal: What characteristics of Christ as "The" Wisdom of God are meaningful to you? Why?

LESSON 2:
DEEPER LEVEL OF WISDOM/OUR BENEFITS

3. What is the deeper level of wisdom (discernment)?

What are all these qualities of wisdom that provide us the privilege of walking on His wonderful path for our lives? What do they mean for us personally?

> "We will know with certainty what He is revealing to us, so we walk on His path, which is best and none better, all for our benefit."

Read Psalm 19:7-14:

7 The law of the Lord is perfect,[a]
   reviving the soul;
the testimony of the Lord is sure,
   making wise the simple;
8 the precepts of the Lord are right,
   rejoicing the heart;
the commandment of the Lord is pure,
   enlightening the eyes;
9 the fear of the Lord is clean,
   enduring forever;
the rules[b] of the Lord are true,
   and righteous altogether.
10 More to be desired are they than gold,
   even much fine gold;
sweeter also than honey
   and drippings of the honeycomb.
11 Moreover, by them is your servant warned;
   in keeping them there is great reward.
12 Who can discern his errors?
   Declare me innocent from hidden faults.
13 Keep back your servant also from presumptuous sins;
   let them not have dominion over me!
Then I shall be blameless,
   and innocent of great transgression.
14 Let the words of my mouth and the meditation of my heart
  be acceptable in your sight,
   O Lord, my rock and my redeemer.

LESSON 2:
DEEPER LEVEL OF WISDOM/OUR BENEFITS

_____
_____
_____
_____
_____

      All of these speak to making things sure, right, pure, enlightened, and leading us to truth. We will know with certainty what He is revealing to us, so we walk on His path, which is best and none better, all for our benefit. It will keep us from presumption – thinking that something is one way when it is something different; or going down a path because it seems obvious when it is not because He knows what is ahead or what is around the corner. All of this is intended to bring us wisdom and give us discernment about which way to go, how to live on a solid base. It will become deeper and deeper and deeper. His revelation to us that we will understand and follow. A wonderful privilege.

Word Definitions: **perfect:** complete, whole, entire, sound, healthful, wholesome, having integrity, what is complete or entirely in accord with truth and fact
converting the soul: to bring back, refresh, restore
sure: made firm, lasting, confirmed, established
wise: teach wisdom, instruct
right: pleasing, correct, straightforward, just, upright, fitting, proper
rejoice: gladden, make glad
pure: clear, sincere, clean (morally, ethically)
enlighten: illuminate, reveal
endure: stand, remain, take one's stand
true: firmness, faithfulness, truth
desire: covet, take pleasure in, delight in
presumptive: arrogant, proud, insolent, presumptuous
dominion: reign, rule over
word: utterance, speech, saying, promise, command
meditation: resounding music, musing
acceptable: pleasure
delight: favor, goodwill, acceptance, will

LESSON 2:
DEEPER LEVEL OF WISDOM/OUR BENEFITS

What is the key to being transformed and proving out His will? Why is that important and how do we practically live this out?

> **Read Romans 12:1-2:**
>
> A Living Sacrifice
> **12** I appeal to you therefore, brothers,[a] by the mercies of God, to present your bodies as a living sacrifice, holy and acceptable to God, which is your spiritual worship.[b] **2** Do not be conformed to this world,[c] but be transformed by the renewal of your mind, that by testing you may discern what is the will of God, what is good and acceptable and perfect.[d]

_____
_____
_____
_____
_____

    We are to offer our body, which is in essence all of us: our soul, our mind, our emotion, our spirit, everything, to serving God, following God, which is our living sacrifice. Sacrifice is putting to death the self. How? By sacrificing our will to His will. He will transform us from the way of the world, from the wisdom of the world. With His wisdom, we will be renewed and be transformed in our mind, so that we can discern the will of God, the real secret. If we try to do it by the world's wisdom, are we going to get the will of God? No. Because it's spiritually discerned to a deeper level of wisdom. This discernment is at the spiritual level, which means we must have the ability to receive it at the spiritual level as opposed to the world's wisdom, which is a logical wisdom.

    To give us His wisdom, He might say, "I know something is coming up, and I can check your spirit by making you uncomfortable about that." Our spouse might say, "I don't know why, but I just don't feel comfortable about this." And again, what is God trying to say? That He knows some wisdom that we don't know and will reveal to us. His will is good, the best. He's trying to protect us from something because He knows something we don't know. Now, that's all spiritual because there's no logic to that, because the answer would be something we cannot see this at the moment. But the Spirit says, "I'm telling you, don't do it." It's a spiritual thing, that's the wisdom of God, and that's what we have to start paying attention to.

LESSON 2:
DEEPER LEVEL OF WISDOM/OUR BENEFITS

We need to sacrifice our will to His will and prove out His will. It is spiritual, not logical. Live in that privilege.

Word Definitions:

living: enjoy real life; to have true life

acceptable: well pleasing

conform: one's self (i.e., one's mind and character) to another's pattern, (fashion one's self according to)

transformed: change into another form, to transform, to transfigure, metamorphosis

renewal: renovation, complete change for the better

mind: comprising alike the faculties of perceiving and understanding and those of feeling, judging, determining

prove (discern): test, recognize as genuine after examination, to approve, deem worthy

good: useful, salutary, pleasant, agreeable, joyful, happy, excellent, distinguished, upright, honorable

acceptable: pleasing

perfect: brought to its end, finished, wanting nothing, necessary to completeness

In these verses, how does this spiritual process work? What does it mean for us to receive His wisdom? How do we live this out practically in our life?

Read 1 Corinthians 2:9-16:

⁹ But, as it is written,
"What no eye has seen, nor ear heard,
　nor the heart of man imagined,
what God has prepared for those who love him"—
¹⁰ these things God has revealed to us through the Spirit. For the Spirit searches everything, even the depths of God. ¹¹ For who knows a person's thoughts except the spirit of that person, which is in him? So also no one comprehends the thoughts of God except the Spirit of God. ¹² Now we have received not the spirit of the world, but the Spirit who is from God, that we might understand the things freely given us by God. ¹³ And we impart this in words not taught by human wisdom but taught by the Spirit, interpreting spiritual truths to those who are spiritual.[a]

LESSON 2:
DEEPER LEVEL OF WISDOM/OUR BENEFITS

> [14] The natural person does not accept the things of the Spirit of God, for they are folly to him, and he is not able to understand them because they are spiritually discerned. [15] The spiritual person judges all things, but is himself to be judged by no one. [16] "For who has understood the mind of the Lord so as to instruct him?" But we have the mind of Christ.

_____
_____
_____
_____

Remember, we have Christ within us. That's where the source of the wisdom comes. And He says, "I give you this wisdom through revelation." He makes known to us things that we didn't know before; disclosed, uncovered. This happens spiritually; not by what we see or hear.

In other words, we cannot get it with our own logic; by our observation or by figuring it out. Maybe we think we can figure things out by analyzing the pros and cons, or that we'll evaluate what we think is good and then decide. He then said we'll get no revelation because we have no ability to get revelation from our senses.

It doesn't say ignore our senses, just subordinate our senses to what He's going to do, which is give us revelation. He's already prepared exactly what He needs to show us in our situations, and He's the one doing it. It's revelation, and it comes spiritually. Who's giving the revelation? God, through the Spirit, and He's resident in us. And we have the mind of Christ.

And we have received that Spirit that freely answers all our questions. Our role is to be receivers. When? Whenever we have a question, or an issue, or a problem. We don't start out saying we've got to go figure this out. Rather, we should go to God and say: "What do You have to say? What are You going to do? I need to be in a position to receive it because You're going to give me the wisdom. And by the way, I expect it and it's going to be spiritually discerned. And I just have to pay attention to the spiritual discernment, because You know more than me, You know what's around the corner, You know things that I don't know, particularly the future or the impact of this decision."

The way we characterize it is that when we're trying to make decisions, we tend to look at the first 10 feet of a 100-mile path. In the first 10 feet, it looks pretty good, so we choose that; and God says: "That's just the first 10 feet of a 100-mile path, and

LESSON 2:
DEEPER LEVEL OF WISDOM/OUR BENEFITS

I know the whole 100 miles. So, if I were you, I'd ask Me. How about if I just tell you which way to go, because you can't possibly figure out the 100-mile path? In that hundred-mile path, there are many ways you can go, but instead of going that way, you really need to go this way."

Further, when we try to figure things out ourselves in the carnal mind (the flesh, the self), we then consider the revelation, the wisdom of God, the Word of God to be foolishness. Why? Because it makes no rational sense. If it doesn't make sense to us, we dismiss it because it seems foolish to consider, not worthwhile. We value our own intellect and the worldly advice higher than God's. So, we reject the spiritual process, that new revelation, that prompting to being uncomfortable, that lack of unity with our spouse because we think we know better. We choose to go with the world because we've considered any spiritual revelation to be foolishness. And we think the world is wise.

And interestingly enough, what happens next is quite comical. We wind up in trouble, which then leads us to believe what?

Well, how did God let us get into trouble? Why did God allow that? Isn't God in control of everything that happens; isn't this God's will? If He really loved us, He would have stopped us from doing it. Well, He actually did. He tried to prompt us through His Spirit. Most people say that they don't even know what that means. That's why this course is so critical. We have to flip from our senses; what we hear or see and process with logic. Again, it's not ignoring that. It's just subordinating that to God's spiritual process. What are we hearing? What do we understand? Pay attention to it because it's discernment.

God is Spirit and communicates to us through His Spirit in us. His ways are not our ways and His thoughts not our thoughts (Isaiah 55:8-11), so since He is Creator and reigns over all, and the material things of this world (including us) were created from the Spiritual (He spoke it from nothing into existence), we and our senses and logic are subordinate to Him, the Spiritual, and the speaking of the Spiritual to us. Our own senses and logic are limited and will operate in the natural, which is based upon observation, evidence, cause and effect, and conclusions. Thus, with this limitation, we are not able to receive what God speaks to us. He says it very strongly: No eye and no ear can receive what He says. What has the Father already done and what is His role? What is our role?

He has prepared in advance what He wishes to reveal to us as He walks us along His path of giving us abundant life and the desires of our hearts. His role is to reveal it (disclose, uncover, make plain, show) and our role is to be a receiver (not striving to understand and get straight, but rather to simply receive willingly what He is speaking to us). It is a spiritual process that happens with the Father speaking to His Spirit in us, who speaks to our soul to communicate what He is saying and what we can understand. He freely gives us this revelation

LESSON 2:
DEEPER LEVEL OF WISDOM/OUR BENEFITS

and continues to speak in ways that we can understand. Thus, as we adults, with our toddler children or grandchildren, do not expect them to have the skills to understand our speech as would another adult, but rather we adjust what and how we say things until they gain understanding—and we love doing it. Our Father is the same way with us.

Word Definitions: **prepared:** make ready, to make the necessary preparations, get everything ready
revealed: disclose, make bare, to make known, make manifest, disclose what before was unknown
things: everything, all things
knows: perceive by any of the senses, to perceive, notice, discern, discover
received: take to one's self, lay hold upon, take possession of, i.e., to appropriate to one's self
freely given: give graciously, give freely, bestow
foolishness: godless, not make sense

What do these verses say is real wisdom? Why is this necessary to live our lives according to God's will?

> **Read 1 Kings 3:5-9:**
>
> [5] At Gibeon the Lord appeared to Solomon in a dream by night, and God said, "Ask what I shall give you."[6] And Solomon said, "You have shown great and steadfast love to your servant David my father, because he walked before you in faithfulness, in righteousness, and in uprightness of heart toward you. And you have kept for him this great and steadfast love and have given him a son to sit on his throne this day. [7] And now, O Lord my God, you have made your servant king in place of David my father, although I am but a little child. I do not know how to go out or come in. [8] And your servant is in the midst of your people whom you have chosen, a great people, too many to be numbered or counted for multitude.[9] Give your servant therefore an understanding mind to govern your people, that I may discern between good and evil, for who is able to govern this your great people?"

_____
_____
_____
_____
_____

LESSON 2:
DEEPER LEVEL OF WISDOM/OUR BENEFITS

God speaks to Solomon and asks him would he wants. Now, Solomon was quite a smart kid and had the equivalent education of having received a Harvard MBA. Additionally he has gained significant knowledge as has sat with his dad, David, in court. He says, "First of all, I'm going to approach every decision as if I don't know the answer. I'm going to approach it as if I'm a little kid because I don't know the answer by definition"—just like us. Why? As we stated before, because we are only seeing 10 feet ahead. We can only perceive what we could understand with our senses and our intellect. And God knows the entire 100-mile path, the bigger picture, and all that He needs to reveal to us about the next steps.

We don't know what's in the future. We don't know what's around the corner. We don't know all the things that He's working to bring about His purposes. We don't know what might have an effect three years later or what might have impact on all kinds of things or all kinds of dimensions that are being set up now with a decision we're going to make. He already knows the answer, both to protect us and to give us the best, and He already knows the impact it will have on what He wants to do for the Kingdom. He's working in all dimensions at once. We need to look at this in a certain way: The domino that we're about ready to hit, hits others all the way downstream and intersects all kinds of other dominoes, so He needed us to hit a certain one. It has impact downstream that either we'll never get to see, or it might be a result that we recognize later, maybe years down the road. We will then understand why He had us do certain things.

Second, he said that he needed an understanding heart—in the Hebrew it is "hearing" heart. He asks God to give him the ability to hear His spiritual insight that he'll need for wisdom so that he can discern between good and evil.

Remember the word "evil" isn't dark, awful, black. Is that hard to discern? No, it's about what looks pretty good to me at the surface. And I we need to know if this is going to turn into something that will annoy, frustrate, irritate, or cause me us trouble downstream. That's what that word means. And He says, give me the hearing heart, because a hearing heart will hear when He'll says: "No, don't do that. Do this. Nope, don't do that now. Don't do that here, do this."

Always seek wisdom and have a heart to hear what God has to say.

Word Definitions:
loved: appetite for
walked: proceed, move, go with
appeared: become visible, present
ask: beg
give: bestow, grant, permit, ascribe, employ, devote, consecrate, dedicate, pay wages
not know: by experience or have wisdom
understanding: hearing, listening with a heart to agree
good: pleasant, agreeable (to the senses); pleasant (to the higher nature), excellent, rich, valuable in estimation

LESSON 2:
DEEPER LEVEL OF WISDOM/OUR BENEFITS

evil: full of labors, annoyances, hardships; pressed and harassed by labors; bringing toils, annoyances, perils; of a time full of peril to Christian faith and steadfastness; causing pain and trouble; bad, of a bad nature or condition; in a
physical sense: diseased or blind
pleased: glad, joyful
discern: hear, listen to, obey; perceive truth
wise: teach wisdom, instruct
riches: wealth
honor: dignity, splendor, reputation

What does this story tell us happened to Joseph regarding his receiving wisdom and how it impacted him? Why is this important to us and how we live our everyday lives?

Read Genesis 41:1-56:

Joseph Interprets Pharaoh's Dreams
41 After two whole years, Pharaoh dreamed that he was standing by the Nile,[2] and behold, there came up out of the Nile seven cows, attractive and plump, and they fed in the reed grass. [3] And behold, seven other cows, ugly and thin, came up out of the Nile after them, and stood by the other cows on the bank of the Nile. [4] And the ugly, thin cows ate up the seven attractive, plump cows. And Pharaoh awoke. [5] And he fell asleep and dreamed a second time. And behold, seven ears of grain, plump and good, were growing on one stalk. [6] And behold, after them sprouted seven ears, thin and blighted by the east wind. [7] And the thin ears swallowed up the seven plump, full ears. And Pharaoh awoke, and behold, it was a dream. [8] So in the morning his spirit was troubled, and he sent and called for all the magicians of Egypt and all its wise men. Pharaoh told them his dreams, but there was none who could interpret them to Pharaoh.

[9] Then the chief cupbearer said to Pharaoh, "I remember my offenses today.[10] When Pharaoh was angry with his servants and put me and the chief baker in custody in the house of the captain of the guard, [11] we dreamed on the same night, he and I, each having a dream with its own interpretation. [12] A young Hebrew was there with us, a servant of the captain of the guard. When we told him, he interpreted our dreams to us, giving an interpretation to each man according to his dream. [13] And as he interpreted to us, so it came about. I was restored to my office, and the baker was hanged."

LESSON 2:
DEEPER LEVEL OF WISDOM/OUR BENEFITS

14 Then Pharaoh sent and called Joseph, and they quickly brought him out of the pit. And when he had shaved himself and changed his clothes, he came in before Pharaoh. 15 And Pharaoh said to Joseph, "I have had a dream, and there is no one who can interpret it. I have heard it said of you that when you hear a dream you can interpret it." 16 Joseph answered Pharaoh, "It is not in me; God will give Pharaoh a favorable answer."[a] 17 Then Pharaoh said to Joseph, "Behold, in my dream I was standing on the banks of the Nile. 18 Seven cows, plump and attractive, came up out of the Nile and fed in the reed grass. 19 Seven other cows came up after them, poor and very ugly and thin, such as I had never seen in all the land of Egypt. 20 And the thin, ugly cows ate up the first seven plump cows,21 but when they had eaten them no one would have known that they had eaten them, for they were still as ugly as at the beginning. Then I awoke. 22 I also saw in my dream seven ears growing on one stalk, full and good. 23 Seven ears, withered, thin, and blighted by the east wind, sprouted after them, 24 and the thin ears swallowed up the seven good ears. And I told it to the magicians, but there was no one who could explain it to me."

25 Then Joseph said to Pharaoh, "The dreams of Pharaoh are one; God has revealed to Pharaoh what he is about to do. 26 The seven good cows are seven years, and the seven good ears are seven years; the dreams are one. 27 The seven lean and ugly cows that came up after them are seven years, and the seven empty ears blighted by the east wind are also seven years of famine. 28 It is as I told Pharaoh; God has shown to Pharaoh what he is about to do. 29 There will come seven years of great plenty throughout all the land of Egypt, 30 but after them there will arise seven years of famine, and all the plenty will be forgotten in the land of Egypt. The famine will consume the land, 31 and the plenty will be unknown in the land by reason of the famine that will follow, for it will be very severe. 32 And the doubling of Pharaoh's dream means that the thing is fixed by God, and God will shortly bring it about. 33 Now therefore let Pharaoh select a discerning and wise man, and set him over the land of Egypt. 34 Let Pharaoh proceed to appoint overseers over the land and take one-fifth of the produce of the land[b] of Egypt during the seven plentiful years. 35 And let them gather all the food of these good years that are coming and store up grain under the authority of Pharaoh for food in the cities, and let them keep it. 36 That food shall be a reserve for the land against the seven years of famine that are to occur in the land of Egypt, so that the land may not perish through the famine."
Joseph Rises to Power

LESSON 2:
DEEPER LEVEL OF WISDOM/OUR BENEFITS

37 This proposal pleased Pharaoh and all his servants. 38 And Pharaoh said to his servants, "Can we find a man like this, in whom is the Spirit of God?"[c] 39 Then Pharaoh said to Joseph, "Since God has shown you all this, there is none so discerning and wise as you are. 40 You shall be over my house, and all my people shall order themselves as you command.[d] Only as regards the throne will I be greater than you." 41 And Pharaoh said to Joseph, "See, I have set you over all the land of Egypt." 42 Then Pharaoh took his signet ring from his hand and put it on Joseph's hand, and clothed him in garments of fine linen and put a gold chain about his neck. 43 And he made him ride in his second chariot. And they called out before him, "Bow the knee!"[e] Thus he set him over all the land of Egypt. 44 Moreover, Pharaoh said to Joseph, "I am Pharaoh, and without your consent no one shall lift up hand or foot in all the land of Egypt." 45 And Pharaoh called Joseph's name Zaphenath-paneah. And he gave him in marriage Asenath, the daughter of Potiphera priest of On. So Joseph went out over the land of Egypt.

46 Joseph was thirty years old when he entered the service of Pharaoh king of Egypt. And Joseph went out from the presence of Pharaoh and went through all the land of Egypt. 47 During the seven plentiful years the earth produced abundantly, 48 and he gathered up all the food of these seven years, which occurred in the land of Egypt, and put the food in the cities. He put in every city the food from the fields around it. 49 And Joseph stored up grain in great abundance, like the sand of the sea, until he ceased to measure it, for it could not be measured.

50 Before the year of famine came, two sons were born to Joseph. Asenath, the daughter of Potiphera priest of On, bore them to him. 51 Joseph called the name of the firstborn Manasseh. "For," he said, "God has made me forget all my hardship and all my father's house."[f] 52 The name of the second he called Ephraim, "For God has made me fruitful in the land of my affliction."[g]
53 The seven years of plenty that occurred in the land of Egypt came to an end, 54 and the seven years of famine began to come, as Joseph had said. There was famine in all lands, but in all the land of Egypt there was bread. 55 When all the land of Egypt was famished, the people cried to Pharaoh for bread. Pharaoh said to all the Egyptians, "Go to Joseph. What he says to you, do."

56 So when the famine had spread over all the land, Joseph opened all the storehouses[h] and sold to the Egyptians, for the famine was severe in the land of Egypt.

LESSON 2:
DEEPER LEVEL OF WISDOM/OUR BENEFITS

_____
_____
_____
_____
_____

Remember what Daniel said, "I get this incredible ability to have this amazing wisdom about dream interpretation, not because of me but because God just gives it to all of His children who have a heart to receive and understand it." Pharaoh chose Joseph, who with the Spirit of God showed us these truths!

So, what was the wisdom, the skill, the gift that God gave Joseph? One of which was dream interpretation. Are we going to have dreams? Sure. A lot of people have dreams. When that happens, what is God doing? Communicating to us by bringing from the unconscious right to the conscious.

Now, why is this such a beautiful thing? We are not engaged, because our eyes and ears and conscious logic aren't in the way. It's now being received purely at a spiritual level. Now that He makes it conscious through our dreams, we must write it down when it is still vivid. If we don't write it down, we'll forget it. Keeping a journal by our beds will allow us to be prepared. When we wake up from a vivid dream, write down all of the important details of the dream. The next morning we can go back, read what we wrote, and remember the dream because we'll have it written down in great detail. The next questions that we ask God are: What does it mean? What message is being given? Is this a warning? Is there something we are to do, or understand, or watch for, or pay attention to?

In Pharaoh's case, the dream was a specific warning with an instruction for what was then to be done in preparation for what was coming.

We have God within us, and there's no system to it. We are to ask Him what it means. It's usually simple, straightforward. What are You trying to say? Ask Him. He's the giver of the wisdom. If it's difficult to understand, there are others who might be able to help. We can ask somebody who is greatly respected: a spouse, a family member, or a close friend. The staff at Living Waters Ministry is also available to help. Remember, dream interpretation is not a special gift. There are not special people with the gifts of interpretation. We all have it because we have the Holy Spirit. Joseph received this and was able to interpret Pharaoh's dream and the warning that was being given. Pharaoh responded and in essence, saved many of his people. God spoke to Pharaoh through a dream and then gave Joseph the wisdom to interpret it. Again, what a privilege.

LESSON 2:
DEEPER LEVEL OF WISDOM/OUR BENEFITS

Word Definitions: **dream:** prophetic
interpretation: understanding the true meaning of dreams
shown: revealed, perceive and see, find out and discern
discerning: understanding, knowing
wise: understanding, receiving teaching and instruction
set over: to give, bestow, grant, permit, ascribe, employ, devote, consecrate

What does this tell us happens when we talk to one another? How is this such a wonderful process for us to receive God's wisdom? How then should we process things together to receive God's wisdom? Why?

Read Malachi 3:16-18:

The Book of Remembrance
¹⁶ Then those who feared the Lord spoke with one another. The Lord paid attention and heard them, and a book of remembrance was written before him of those who feared the Lord and esteemed his name. ¹⁷ "They shall be mine, says the Lord of hosts, in the day when I make up my treasured possession, and I will spare them as a man spares his son who serves him. ¹⁸ Then once more you shall see the distinction between the righteous and the wicked, between one who serves God and one who does not serve him.

_____
_____
_____
_____
_____

    We actually discovered this on one of our retreats. While we're talking to each other, we know God is listening to us. It's an interesting form of prayer. Why we're processing, because we're seeking wisdom, we share what we are hearing; what we are understanding. So, keep talking about it. And the more we talk about it while we're doing that, we are praying because He's listening. He says: While we're talking, we are openly seeking God for clarity: "I wonder what that means; I wonder

LESSON 2:
DEEPER LEVEL OF WISDOM/OUR BENEFITS

what else we need to know. I wonder what God's going to show us. I wonder why that's not coming together."

He says, "I know you want to know that. Let Me give you the discernment to tell you the difference between righteous and unrighteous, between what's right and what's not, between good and not good." As we dialogue about the very issues we have and continue to openly share, ask: What do we think, feel, and believe? What are we understanding? We, then, also are receiving whatever the Spirit is confirming or not confirming on this. Are we at odds with this? Are we feeling uncomfortable with this? Are we receiving insight about this? He says, "Discernment comes through the dialogue."

And then suddenly when we're talking about it, something wonderful happens: "Did you realize what you just said? Oh, my gosh, there's a piece of the puzzle." It's amazing. And it happens all the time.

Then, we process that further and receive additional insight as we experience God revealing the difference between what is right or not; what is His will or not. We will find this to be an amazing process that we need to embrace and enjoy.

Word Definitions: **discern:** see, observe, consider, look at, give attention to, receive
righteous: (as justified and vindicated by God), right, correct, lawful
wicked: hostile, enmity against God
serve: surrendered to the rule of (either God, or self)

Write in journal: Regarding your issues and questions: What discernment are you receiving that helps you understand the truth and thus God's will better?

4. **What are the benefits of this wisdom to us?**

What do these verses list as benefits to receiving wisdom? How might we apply these to our everyday lives?

> **Read Proverbs 3:13-18:**
>
> Blessed Is the One Who Finds Wisdom
> ¹³ Blessed is the one who finds wisdom,
>   and the one who gets understanding,
> ¹⁴ for the gain from her is better than gain from silver
>   and her profit better than gold.
> ¹⁵ She is more precious than jewels,

LESSON 2:
DEEPER LEVEL OF WISDOM/OUR BENEFITS

> and nothing you desire can compare with her.
> ¹⁶ Long life is in her right hand;
>   in her left hand are riches and honor.
> ¹⁷ Her ways are ways of pleasantness,
>   and all her paths are peace.
> ¹⁸ She is a tree of life to those who lay hold of her;
>   those who hold her fast are called blessed.

_____
_____
_____
_____
_____

Walking in wisdom provides us with wonderful benefits, starting with how we will be blessed: an all-encompassing Word of God's goodness in our lives. This brings:

1. Shalom—great favor

2. Paths that are pleasant, even delightful. Which paths? All our paths, always.

This means we'll be walking in shalom, with God's favor. We will be walking in pleasantness, in delight. We must ask whether or not something is leading us to pleasantness. And if it's not, don't go down that path. And secondly, if we're not on that path, then we need to recognize that and acknowledge that something's not right. We need to get on the right path, the benefit of being on that path is great peace/favor and pleasantness. Blessedness is freedom and joy of being on His path, which He brings to us.

Word Definitions: **happy:** blessedness, go straight, advance
wisdom: skill (in war), wisdom (in administration), shrewdness
prudence: to be made wise
understanding: insight, discernment

By walking in wisdom, who is the recipient of wisdom? What does this mean, and why is this important?

LESSON 2:
DEEPER LEVEL OF WISDOM/OUR BENEFITS

> **Read Proverbs 9:10-12:**
>
> ^{10} The fear of the Lord is the beginning of wisdom,
>   and the knowledge of the Holy One is insight.
> ^{11} For by me your days will be multiplied,
>   and years will be added to your life.
> ^{12} If you are wise, you are wise for yourself;
>   if you scoff, you alone will bear it.

_____
_____
_____
_____

    If we're wise, we are wise for ourselves. In other words, He's saying the biggest benefit is wisdom that is not generic and not philosophical. If we seek wisdom, guess what? We will benefit personally. So, seek wisdom!

Word Definitions: **fear:** respect
                             reverence: looks to Him and knows that what He says is true

As we live in His wisdom, what does that do for us? How important is that for living a life of stability and security? Why?

> **Read Proverbs 14:26-27:**
>
> ^{26} In the fear of the Lord one has strong confidence,
>   and his children will have a refuge.
> ^{27} The fear of the Lord is a fountain of life,
>   that one may turn away from the snares of death.

_____
_____
_____
_____

LESSON 2:
DEEPER LEVEL OF WISDOM/OUR BENEFITS

With wisdom comes this amazing confidence. What is that? Confidence in assurance. He spoke and we heard; therefore, it's going to happen. Things go well for us. Our trust is in God and we respond to what He's saying and walk in the discernment that He's giving us. I'm confident in what He says and the path that He has shown will happen.

So, when He says to us, "Don't make that investment," does it make sense? It's against all the worldly wisdom. What confidence do we have? He knows more than we do, and therefore we'll be blessed if we stay with Him. We are to do this and not look back. Because He said it, we should do it. We may not yet understand the impact of it, but it's going to work. Have confidence. Don't second guess it. Don't get wishy washy and say: "I wonder if I made a mistake. I wonder." No, have confidence because God already has shown us the way.

Confidence builds as we keep trusting. It gets easier and easier. Go back and look at these markers. He's always faithful. Keep recording and remembering that He is always faithful. He wants to have us live in this confidence. It gives us security and safety and stability.

Word Definitions:

strong: prevailing, might
confidence: to be bold, to be secure

If we live in wisdom, what follows us? Why is that such a wonderful place to live?

> **Read Proverbs 16:20-21:**
>
> 20 Whoever gives thought to the word[a] will discover good,
>   and blessed is he who trusts in the Lord.
> 21 The wise of heart is called discerning,
>   and sweetness of speech increases persuasiveness.

_____
_____
_____
_____

As we receive discernment, the happier we'll be. We will be receiving and speaking the delight of life, what we are learning we will be living out. We're going to get more wisdom and goodness will follow us. Blessedness.

LESSON 2:
DEEPER LEVEL OF WISDOM/OUR BENEFITS

Word Definition: **good:** pleasant, agreeable (to the senses); pleasant (to the higher nature), excellent, rich, valuable in estimation, glad, happy, prosperous

With wisdom, what will we live in and not experience? What does that mean to us in our lives, personally?

> **Read Proverbs 19:8; 23:**
>
> ⁸ Whoever gets sense loves his own soul;
>   he who keeps understanding will discover good.
>
> ²³ The fear of the Lord leads to life,
>   and whoever has it rests satisfied;
>   he will not be visited by harm.

_____
_____
_____
_____
_____

We will have a life of satisfaction, of fullness, one that will not be visited with evil. It doesn't mean it won't happen to us. It means annoying, frustrating, irritating things will not occupy our life as a way of life. It will only be temporary, as wisdom will lead us to satisfaction and fullness. We will enjoy His path of pleasantness and shalom and be in His favor. Wonderful benefits.

Word Definitions: **abide:** dwell, remain in, pass the night in
satisfaction: be fulfilled, be filled, abounding
evil: bad, disagreeable, malignant; unpleasant, giving pain, unhappiness, misery; displeasing; not valuable, sad, unhappy, hurtful

LESSON 2:
DEEPER LEVEL OF WISDOM/OUR BENEFITS

What in these verses are all the benefits listed of receiving wisdom? What do these mean to us in our everyday lives?

> **Read Proverbs 2:5-10:**
>
> 5 then you will understand the fear of the Lord
>   and find the knowledge of God.
> 6 For the Lord gives wisdom;
>   from his mouth come knowledge and understanding;
> 7 he stores up sound wisdom for the upright;
>   he is a shield to those who walk in integrity,
> 8 guarding the paths of justice
>   and watching over the way of his saints.
> 9 Then you will understand righteousness and justice
>   and equity, every good path;
> 10 for wisdom will come into your heart,
>   and knowledge will be pleasant to your soul;

_____
_____
_____
_____

    When we receive His wisdom, we live in righteousness, equity, justice, all this is good. Our paths will all be good, because they will be led by His wisdom. The good word here is "best": excellent, spectacular, supernatural, miraculous. We'll live there because we'll know it and walk in every good path that He has planned out for us. The benefit of having wisdom is that God says: "I know every single good path for you. And the benefit of living in My wisdom is what? That it's good, it's good, it's good."

    In the context of living in the world, we're going to have difficulties. He's not removing us from these. But He will resolve all these difficulties and give us His path of wisdom, a path that is spectacular. He wants to show us that, and to give us an opportunity to enjoy life and have joy in life. And it's all of this together. It's not limited to financial things or material things. It's all the aspects of life that give us the joy of life. And that wisdom will walk on this path as He shows us how to handle the things of life that each of us must deal with.

LESSON 2:
DEEPER LEVEL OF WISDOM/OUR BENEFITS

Word Definitions: **equity:** pleasing, be agreeable, be right
good: pleasant, agreeable (to the senses); pleasant (to the higher nature), excellent, rich, valuable in estimation: glad, happy, prosperous
path: track to run on

Write in journal: What benefits have you recently experienced? How? What benefits have you not recently experienced? Why?

LESSON 3:
HOW DO WE RECEIVE THIS WISDOM?

5. How do we receive this wisdom?

What are the two keys to receiving wisdom, as Solomon asked for? What does that look like in our personal life?

> **Read 1 Kings 3:3-14:**
>
> **3** Solomon loved the Lord, walking in the statutes of David his father, only he sacrificed and made offerings at the high places. **4** And the king went to Gibeon to sacrifice there, for that was the great high place. Solomon used to offer a thousand burnt offerings on that altar. **5** At Gibeon the Lord appeared to Solomon in a dream by night, and God said, "Ask what I shall give you." **6** And Solomon said, "You have shown great and steadfast love to your servant David my father, because he walked before you in faithfulness, in righteousness, and in uprightness of heart toward you. And you have kept for him this great and steadfast love and have given him a son to sit on his throne this day. **7** And now, O Lord my God, you have made your servant king in place of David my father, although I am but a little child. I do not know how to go out or come in. **8** And your servant is in the midst of your people whom you have chosen, a great people, too many to be numbered or counted for multitude. **9** Give your servant therefore an understanding mind to govern your people, that I may discern between good and evil, for who is able to govern this your great people?"
>
> **10** It pleased the Lord that Solomon had asked this. **11** And God said to him, "Because you have asked this, and have not asked for yourself long life or riches or the life of your enemies, but have asked for yourself understanding to discern what is right, **12** behold, I now do according to your word. Behold, I give you a wise and discerning mind, so that none like you has been before you and none like you shall arise after you. **13** I

> "We need that discernment that is spiritual and not logical. We will need the ability to increase our sensitivity, and the ability to hear better. This is what is needed and what we should pray for."

LESSON 3:
HOW DO WE RECEIVE THIS WISDOM?

> give you also what you have not asked, both riches and honor, so that no other king shall compare with you, all your days.[14] And if you will walk in my ways, keeping my statutes and my commandments, as your father David walked, then I will lengthen your days."

_____
_____
_____
_____

We have already looked at this regarding the definition of wisdom. Remember, there were two significant points. Solomon said: "I'm approaching every decision as if I'm a child; as if I don't know because I don't know that 100-mile path, and I can only see the first 10 feet. You know what's around the corner, You know the future. So, by definition, I need Your wisdom all the time. I'm going to approach it that way." And then also, he said: "Give me an understanding heart, a hearing heart so that I can discern between things that are fuzzy to me, that are gray to me, that look pretty good to me, or that I am unsure about. In the natural, I can choose something that seems okay to me, but You're going to give me the discernment of exactly which path to take if I pay attention in the Spirit." And what do we need for that? A heart to hear what He's going to say to us. We need that discernment that is spiritual and not logical. We will need the ability to increase our sensitivity, and the ability to hear better. This is what is needed and what we should pray for.

Word Definitions:

loved: appetite for
walked: proceed, move, go with
appeared: become visible, present
ask: beg
give: bestow, grant, permit, ascribe, employ, devote, consecrate, dedicate, pay wages
not know: by experience or have wisdom
understanding: hearing, listening with a heart to agree
good: pleasant, agreeable (to the senses); pleasant (to the higher nature), excellent, rich, valuable in estimation, glad, happy, prosperous
evil: bad, disagreeable, malignant; unpleasant, giving pain, unhappiness, misery; displeasing; not valuable, sad, unhappy, hurtful

LESSON 3:
HOW DO WE RECEIVE THIS WISDOM?

pleased: glad, joyful
discern: hear, listen to, obey; perceive truth
wise: understanding, receiving teaching and instruction
riches: wealth
honor: dignity, splendor, reputation

What does David say is important for him to receive wisdom? What does that look like for each of us personally?

> **Read Psalm 51:16-19:**
>
> 16 For you will not delight in sacrifice, or I would give it;
>   you will not be pleased with a burnt offering.
> 17 The sacrifices of God are a broken spirit;
>   a broken and contrite heart, O God, you will not despise.
> 18 Do good to Zion in your good pleasure;
>   build up the walls of Jerusalem;
> 19 then will you delight in right sacrifices,
>   in burnt offerings and whole burnt offerings;
>   then bulls will be offered on your altar.

_____
_____
_____
_____
_____

    David understood that the key to wisdom is not religious activities, a religious system; rather, God is looking for us to seek Him with an open heart. We need to be contrite, which is very simple. We need to follow Him completely and fully. We are not going to be prideful and decide that we know better.

LESSON 3:
HOW DO WE RECEIVE THIS WISDOM?

This plays out in our lives and our decisions, and in how we process decisions. Are we seeking God's way or do we just follow our own decisions? Do we even think about it? Does God have a way for this since He has an answer for this? A lot of people don't even know or think that He does.

How many decisions does He want to show us? All of them. He's not asking us to make the big decisions while He handles the small ones. Or vice versa. This is where people get in trouble. We think we've heard God tell us this, and we then followed that. And then from that point forward, we just did what we wanted to do, and we wind up in deep trouble. And then we wonder why God allowed us to get into this trouble. Just because we follow Him in His first instruction doesn't mean that He will bless us no matter what. By not continuing to follow Him and seek His wisdom, His answers, we will have caused the adversity ourselves because we think that God is just the God of the big things. No, it's everything along the way. Remember, Christ said: "I did nothing except what the Father told me. And I'll direct you and give you wisdom and give you insight about everything you're doing."

With the decisions we're about to make, do we have confirmation when the decision is bigger than us? If the decision involves others (i.e., a decision with a spouse, a decision for our families, decisions regarding our marriages, decisions with ministry partners, etc.), decisions bigger than us, by definition, do the others involved have confirmation in their spirit about these decisions? Do they have agreement with us? Are we seeking God together? It's as simple as asking, "Hey, honey, this affects us. How do you feel about hiring this guy today? We're going to hire this housekeeper to do this work. Do you feel good about it? Yeah, I feel good about it. A great hire wasn't a big deal. We didn't spend hours and hours and hours praying. Do we have to go search every housekeeper there is? Why would we? We had one walk through the door. We interviewed her but do we feel good in your spirit about this? Do we feel at peace about this? You feel that. God's confirming that. Great. Let's hire." It became fairly simple.

Here's an example: You're going to go have a bowl of cereal. You do not stand in front of the opened cupboard and ask God, "Which of these boxes of cereal should I eat today?" You're just going to go pick one. You pick one and start walking to the kitchen, and God says: "Don't eat it." Now, normally He doesn't say anything about your choice in cereals. But this time He says, "Don't eat it." Pay attention. He interrupted you because there's something about it, there's something that happened to it. You hear God's Word, you follow His instruction, and you do not eat it. What you don't do is question Him by asking: "Should I, should I, should I?" God interrupted you. It was a normal choice that you're making about things that you normally make every single day. He doesn't have a desire to neurotically have you choose this today and that tomorrow because it doesn't really matter per se. On this particular day though, it mattered. Don't eat that cereal.

LESSON 3:
HOW DO WE RECEIVE THIS WISDOM?

There is no system, because it is a relationship with Him, and our role is to have a contrite heart—a willingness to always follow Him in relationship and follow Him leading and guiding us.

Word Definitions:
- **acknowledge:** recognize, admit, confess
- **create:** shape, form
- **clean:** pure
- **renew:** make anew, repair
- **restore:** refresh, repair
- **joy:** gladness
- **salvation:** deliverance, welfare, prosperity, wholeness

What do these verses say about Solomon's heart? What does that mean and how do we apply this to our lives?

> **Read 1 Kings 4:29-30:**
>
> [29] And God gave Solomon wisdom and understanding beyond measure, and breadth of mind like the sand on the seashore, [30] so that Solomon's wisdom surpassed the wisdom of all the people of the east and all the wisdom of Egypt.

_____
_____
_____
_____
_____

As God was giving Solomon wisdom and exceeding understanding, He gave him largeness of heart, the ability to be open to receive whatever He's going to show him. Solomon didn't limit Him, or box God in, or put Him in a little system. He was open to God telling him things that were going to blow his mind—and get bigger and bigger. These will not be natural things but spiritual things—wonderful revelations that will not be limited by our thinking, by our restrictions. God will enlarge our hearts to receive His goodness. We need to ask for this.

Word Definitions: **largeness:** roomy pasture, be enlarged

LESSON 3:
HOW DO WE RECEIVE THIS WISDOM?

What happened when the Queen of Sheba came and visited Solomon? How do we receive this regarding God giving us wisdom and applying this to our lives?

Read 2 Chronicles 9:1-12; 22-23:

The Queen of Sheba

9 Now when the queen of Sheba heard of the fame of Solomon, she came to Jerusalem to test him with hard questions, having a very great retinue and camels bearing spices and very much gold and precious stones. And when she came to Solomon, she told him all that was on her mind. **2** And Solomon answered all her questions. There was nothing hidden from Solomon that he could not explain to her. **3** And when the queen of Sheba had seen the wisdom of Solomon, the house that he had built, **4** the food of his table, the seating of his officials, and the attendance of his servants, and their clothing, his cupbearers, and their clothing, and his burnt offerings that he offered at the house of the Lord, there was no more breath in her.

5 And she said to the king, "The report was true that I heard in my own land of your words and of your wisdom, **6** but I did not believe the[a] reports until I came and my own eyes had seen it. And behold, half the greatness of your wisdom was not told me; you surpass the report that I heard. **7** Happy are your wives![b] Happy are these your servants, who continually stand before you and hear your wisdom! 8 Blessed be the Lord your God, who has delighted in you and set you on his throne as king for the Lord your God! Because your God loved Israel and would establish them forever, he has made you king over them, that you may execute justice and righteousness." **9** Then she gave the king 120 talents[c] of gold, and a very great quantity of spices, and precious stones. There were no spices such as those that the queen of Sheba gave to King Solomon.

10 Moreover, the servants of Hiram and the servants of Solomon, who brought gold from Ophir, brought algum wood and precious stones. **11** And the king made from the algum wood supports for the house of the Lord and for the king's house, lyres also and harps for the singers. There never was seen the like of them before in the land of Judah.

12 And King Solomon gave to the queen of Sheba all that she desired, whatever she asked besides what she had brought to the king. So she turned and went back to her own land with her servants.

LESSON 3:
HOW DO WE RECEIVE THIS WISDOM?

_____

_____

_____

_____

_____

When the Queen of Sheba heard of the famous Solomon, she came to Jerusalem to test Solomon with hard questions. She came with a great retinue, camels, horses, spices, gold, and precious stones. She spoke with him about all that was in her heart. Solomon answered all the questions. There was nothing so difficult for Solomon that he could not speak to her.

How many of her hard questions—all that were in her heart—did Solomon answer? All of them. God does the same for us. God says: "It's really pretty simple, give Me your best shot. Ask Me anything. Give Me the hardest questions you have – I will give you wisdom for all of them."

It is best not to stop asking for His guidance, particularly when we are struggling for understanding or have only a piece of the puzzle; or when we have an enigma or a conundrum that has no easy answer. We all have problems that we don't see a way through. It's a riddle, it's an enigma, it's a conundrum, because every time we make decisions on our own, it turns out badly. Or maybe we have a dilemma, and we can't see an answer to it. What does God say? To bring it on! Bring it to Him as nothing is too difficult for Him. He has answers to every issue we have.

And remember, God says there's one thing we're forgetting: His answers aren't natural. When Moses is at the Red Sea and Pharaoh and his men were chasing him down, as far as he was concerned, it was over. But God had an interesting solution to that, one that we certainly would not have thought of.

How about Jehoshaphat with all the nations coming against the people of Judah?" He had no solution but went to God and asked for help. God said: "The battle is not yours but Mine. Go down there and watch what I'm about ready to do," The enemy armies wind up killing each other—this was God's spiritual answer to Jehoshaphat's most difficult problem.

Ask Him the hardest questions we have. He will give us the answers.

Word Definitions: **commune:** speak with one another, talk
stand: abide, remain, persist, endure
hear: listen to, obey, perceive truth
delighted: take pleasure in
sought: seek to find

LESSON 3:
HOW DO WE RECEIVE THIS WISDOM?

What are the activities that are our responsibilities as we pursue wisdom? What do these look like in our lives?

> **Read Proverbs 2:1-4:**
>
> The Value of Wisdom
> **2** My son, if you receive my words
>   and treasure up my commandments with you,
> ² making your ear attentive to wisdom
>   and inclining your heart to understanding;
> ³ yes, if you call out for insight
>   and raise your voice for understanding,
> ⁴ if you seek it like silver
>   and search for it as for hidden treasures,

_____
_____
_____
_____
_____

    These verses tell us to go after wisdom with everything we've got. Keep going, keep going, don't quit, don't give up. Search for it as if it's a hidden treasure. Why? Because He has our answers. So, if we were staying in a house and were told there are gold bars hidden in there, what would we do? Turn it upside down. We search for it because we know the treasure is there. We don't know exactly where it is, but we know it's there. That's what He's saying. Wisdom is there. Keep going until we get the answer.

    Don't quit too early, and don't say, well, it's unknowable. It's there. Go after it. Go after it. Go after it. By the way, consider that it will be piece by piece by piece; it doesn't have to be all at once, even though our desire is for Him to give us the whole thing and skip all the in-between stuff. He said: "I'll give it to you piece by piece."

    As we have explained before, sometimes God will withhold bits of the answer because the timing isn't right. Though we are in a big hurry, He isn't. His timing is perfect, and He will reveal what we need to know in His timing. This goes back to confidence. Be confident that He'll make that known in the proper time and realize that He's working many sides of this. It just hasn't yet clicked into our gear.

LESSON 3:
HOW DO WE RECEIVE THIS WISDOM?

The key is to keep going, pursue it all the time until we receive the answers we need. He will give it and wants us to always pursue this until we receive it.

Word Definition: **receive:** to take as own, get, fetch, lay hold of, seize

As we are receiving wisdom, what is important for us to receive it? How do we apply this in our everyday lives?

> **Read Proverbs 4:1-9; 20-23:**
>
> A Father's Wise Instruction
> **4** Hear, O sons, a father's instruction,
>   and be attentive, that you may gain[a] insight,
> ² for I give you good precepts;
>   do not forsake my teaching.
> ³ When I was a son with my father,
>   tender, the only one in the sight of my mother,
> ⁴ he taught me and said to me,
> "Let your heart hold fast my words;
>   keep my commandments, and live.
> ⁵ Get wisdom; get insight;
>   do not forget, and do not turn away from the words of my mouth.
> ⁶ Do not forsake her, and she will keep you;
>   love her, and she will guard you.
> ⁷ The beginning of wisdom is this: Get wisdom,
>   and whatever you get, get insight.
> ⁸ Prize her highly, and she will exalt you;
>   she will honor you if you embrace her.
> ⁹ She will place on your head a graceful garland;
>   she will bestow on you a beautiful crown."
>
> ²⁰ My son, be attentive to my words;
>   incline your ear to my sayings.
> ²¹ Let them not escape from your sight;
>   keep them within your heart.
> ²² For they are life to those who find them,
>   and healing to all their[a] flesh.
> ²³ Keep your heart with all vigilance,
>   for from it flow the springs of life.

LESSON 3:
HOW DO WE RECEIVE THIS WISDOM?

_____
_____
_____
_____
_____

As we are receiving wisdom, we are to pay attention to the words being spoken to us by God. We are thus listening, abiding, hearing. God will say things, and suddenly it will strike our heart. We are then to acknowledge it and pay attention. In the moment when we hear it, we might not fully understand all that it means, other than it registered. He's leading us down a path so listen closely to what He says. He sets it up as a treasure hunt, and we are to pay attention to the clues.

God will give us the clues, and suddenly, we will see what that means. And then we go to the next part of the map on the treasure hunt and eventually will see what that means, too. In the Nicolas Cage movie, National Treasure, the characters keep getting more and more clues to find the treasure. They had to follow clues and each time, instead of finding the treasure, they found another clue. This went on and on They had to pay close attention to finding the clues, because missing one would derail their search. Only after following all of the clues did they find their treasure.

This is what God is saying to us. "I'm taking you on a kind of treasure hunt, and there's joy to this, so pay attention; I have something to show you. There's new information, and you're getting insight, and you're getting clarity. Eventually you'll get the final answer you seek. Pay attention, pay attention, pay attention."

Word Definitions: **retain:** to grasp, hold, support, attain, lay hold of, hold fast
attend: pay attention, take heed to
keep: guard, protect

As we are paying attention, what are the three things we are to do to receive the answers? What does that look like in our everyday lives?

> **Read Proverbs 8:32-35:**
>
> [32] "And now, O sons, listen to me:
>   blessed are those who keep my ways.
> [33] Hear instruction and be wise,
>   and do not neglect it.

LESSON 3:
HOW DO WE RECEIVE THIS WISDOM?

> ³⁴ Blessed is the one who listens to me,
>   watching daily at my gates,
>   waiting beside my doors.
> ³⁵ For whoever finds me finds life
>   and obtains favor from the Lord,

_____

_____

_____

_____

_____

He tells us to listen, watch, wait.

- Listening: What are You saying, God? Help us understand the insight, the discernment, the truth.

- Watching: Stay on alert and observe. Be on alert and look for what happens next.

- Waiting: not acting on our own until we have confirmation that we know what God knows. Actively pursue the knowing until we have the answer from God: waiting on the answer and not acting on our own.

Listen, watch, wait. All three work together to help us stay in process until we receive His answer.

Word Definition: **blessed:** happiness
listens: hears, yield to, obey, be obedient
watching: be alert
waiting: keep, guard, dance with
life: flowing, fresh (of water), lively, active (of man), reviving
favor: pleasure, delight, goodwill, acceptance

LESSON 3:
HOW DO WE RECEIVE THIS WISDOM?

When there are points where we are stuck in the process or not sure of the answer, what are we to consider? What kind of advisers do we include in the process with us? How does this work in our decision-making process?

> **Read Proverbs 11:14; 15:22:**
>
> [14] Where there is no guidance, a people falls,
>   but in an abundance of counselors there is safety.
>
> [22] Without counsel plans fail,
>   but with many advisers they succeed.

_____
_____
_____
_____
_____

As we're walking down the path seeking wisdom, sometimes we need some outside help, either because we are stuck in the process and not sure how to proceed any further or because we are unsure of the answer. We need two types of counselors:

1. A godly counselor: regarding the definition of wisdom, how would we define a godly counselor? One who doesn't give us the answer, but instead says they will go with us in the same process we are going through, and together we will seek God for the answer. We don't want somebody who's a Christian to give us worldly wisdom since God's wisdom is spiritually discerned. We aren't looking for worldly wisdom. We want somebody who is going to walk with us to seek God's wisdom and spiritual discernment, to help with the process of seeking and help with confirmation. We can ask: "What are you hearing?" They have the same Holy Spirit and can confirm or let us know that they aren't sure so the process should keep going. We should seek it together. They can ask questions and give us some thoughts. Through dialogue they can assist us in the process.

2. A technical counselor: an expert who is neutral; usually a technical expert. Someone who knows more than we do, because we are dealing with an issue that is beyond our expertise, our understanding of something for which

LESSON 3:
HOW DO WE RECEIVE THIS WISDOM?

we need technical input. This should be from somebody who's completely neutral and doesn't care about the outcome at all. They can offer truth with no prejudice. We can find somebody who's an absolute expert on this particular issue that we're trying to get wisdom about, someone who will give the truth with no vested interest. This is likely someone we would pay.

Do not be afraid to get some help when needed. It is an important part of the process and can bring us what is needed during those times we are either stuck in the process or need further confirmation of the truth.

Word Definitions: **counselors:** advisors, consultants
safety: salvation, deliverance
disappointed: broken, frustrated
established: fixed, confirmed

Since receiving wisdom is a spiritual process, how does this spiritual process work? How do we apply this to our lives?

> **Read 1 Corinthians 2:9-12:**
>
> ⁹ But, as it is written,
> "What no eye has seen, nor ear heard,
> nor the heart of man imagined,
> what God has prepared for those who love him"—
> ¹⁰ these things God has revealed to us through the Spirit. For the Spirit searches everything, even the depths of God. ¹¹ For who knows a person's thoughts except the spirit of that person, which is in him? So also no one comprehends the thoughts of God except the Spirit of God. ¹² Now we have received not the spirit of the world, but the Spirit who is from God, that we might understand the things freely given us by God.

_____
_____
_____
_____
_____

LESSON 3:
HOW DO WE RECEIVE THIS WISDOM?

We have reviewed this previously. Wisdom is spiritually discerned. It's revelation. We must be receivers. We do not figure things out with our own intellect by what we see and hear with our senses. Rather, we must always be in a position of subordinating our intellect, our logic to the spiritual process of receiving by listening, processing, understanding God's revelation to us, which He will give.

Word Definitions: **prepared:** make ready, get everything ready
revealed: disclosed, uncovered, make known
received: to take upon one's self, to take in order to carry away
know: experience, receive

In seeking wisdom, what are we to do and have settled in order for us to receive it? What does this mean to us personally?

> **Read James 1:5-8:**
> [5] If any of you lacks wisdom, let him ask God, who gives generously to all without reproach, and it will be given him. [6] But let him ask in faith, with no doubting, for the one who doubts is like a wave of the sea that is driven and tossed by the wind. [7] For that person must not suppose that he will receive anything from the Lord; [8] he is a double-minded man, unstable in all his ways.

_____
_____
_____
_____
_____

    This lays out the process clearly. We lack wisdom (about everything), so we are to ask God, who is committed to giving us this wisdom (answers) liberally and with great clarity to us. We must believe either that He will give us this wisdom, or He will not give us the wisdom. We must have this settled. We can't say we're seeking wisdom, even though we don't believe He will get it to us. We must be sure. Don't believe that we can't hear it properly because we're not as spiritually attuned as somebody else; or have not experienced it before; or just aren't sure about all this. God says, "I'll get it to you. Just ask Me. The most immature believer can get the answer. I'll get it to you in a way you can understand it. You just have to ask Me and get settled that I will get you the answer, you must believe this. That's a condition.

LESSON 3:
HOW DO WE RECEIVE THIS WISDOM?

Keep asking, keep asking, keep asking, and I'll get it to you. Just listen, watch, and wait. I'll get it to you."

Word Definitions: **ask:** beg, call for, crave, desire, require
liberally: simply, openly, frankly, sincerely
faith: conviction of the truth of anything, belief
doubting: to oppose, strive with dispute, contend

In these verses, what is our prayer as we seek wisdom? What does all this mean to us personally?

> **Read Ephesians 1:16-21:**
>
> [16] I do not cease to give thanks for you, remembering you in my prayers, [17] that the God of our Lord Jesus Christ, the Father of glory, may give you the Spirit of wisdom and of revelation in the knowledge of him, [18] having the eyes of your hearts enlightened, that you may know what is the hope to which he has called you, what are the riches of his glorious inheritance in the saints, [19] and what is the immeasurable greatness of his power toward us who believe, according to the working of his great might [20] that he worked in Christ when he raised him from the dead and seated him at his right hand in the heavenly places, [21] far above all rule and authority and power and dominion, and above every name that is named, not only in this age but also in the one to come.

_____
_____
_____
_____
_____

These verses say to pray specifically for wisdom, revelation, knowledge, and understanding; and it will come with His power to deliver it. If we pray for it, ask for it—He will give it to us.

LESSON 3:
HOW DO WE RECEIVE THIS WISDOM?

Word Definitions: **wisdom:** manage affairs with God's perspective, interpret things spiritually
revelation: disclosing things not known naturally, laying open, laying bare
knowledge: correct truth
understanding: thoughts and emotions (heart, soul) getting it
enlighten: give light, clarity
hope: confident and expectation
calling: invitation to feast
riches: wealth
honor: dignity, riches, abundance
glory: splendor, beauty
inheritance: possession
power: (dunamis) authority
toward: ours to have
power: external force, mighty, might, to do, authority; power (exousia), governing power

What else are we to pray? How does this apply to our lives?

Read Colossians 1: 9-12:

⁹ And so, from the day we heard, we have not ceased to pray for you, asking that you may be filled with the knowledge of his will in all spiritual wisdom and understanding, ¹⁰ so as to walk in a manner worthy of the Lord, fully pleasing to him: bearing fruit in every good work and increasing in the knowledge of God; ¹¹ being strengthened with all power, according to his glorious might, for all endurance and patience with joy; ¹² giving thanks[a] to the Father, who has qualified you[b] to share in the inheritance of the saints in light.

_____
_____
_____
_____

LESSON 3:
HOW DO WE RECEIVE THIS WISDOM?

We continue to pray that we are filled with the knowledge that He will reveal to us, so that we will understand with wisdom, His will, His answers for us. We don't pray that someone else will give us answers, or that we guess right, or that God will bless us with worldly answers. Instead, we pray that we have a heart to receive God's answer, that we are not stubborn or self-centered, that we don't think we know better. We pray that we hear those things, that our eyes are open, that we understand step by step, and that we continue to seek it until we understand His will. He will deliver it to us—spiritually.

Word Definitions: **longsuffering:** patience, endurance, perseverance
joy: gladness

As we receive wisdom, what does He tell us is a quality that helps reach confirmation? How does this work in our everyday decision making?

> **Read Colossians 3:12-17:**
>
> [12] Put on then, as God's chosen ones, holy and beloved, compassionate hearts, kindness, humility, meekness, and patience, [13] bearing with one another and, if one has a complaint against another, forgiving each other; as the Lord has forgiven you, so you also must forgive. [14] And above all these put on love, which binds everything together in perfect harmony. [15] And let the peace of Christ rule in your hearts, to which indeed you were called in one body. And be thankful. [16] Let the word of Christ dwell in you richly, teaching and admonishing one another in all wisdom, singing psalms and hymns and spiritual songs, with thankfulness in your hearts to God. [17] And whatever you do, in word or deed, do everything in the name of the Lord Jesus, giving thanks to God the Father through him.

_____
_____
_____
_____
_____

LESSON 3:
HOW DO WE RECEIVE THIS WISDOM?

He says: "Let peace/shalom rule in your hearts." The word "rule" means umpire—determine if we are receiving God's will, His answer, His wisdom. Are we at peace with His wisdom? Do we have it or is He troubling us? Is He saying, 'No, we don't have it?' Or are we feeling there's something not right? An umpire determines in or out, fair or foul, right or wrong. That's also how we operate. It's a spiritual thing. We pay attention to that. We don't have to know why this umpire is ruling this way at the moment, just that we are either having confirmation or need to go farther because we haven't received confirmation. Our spouses can join us in this. If they aren't receiving confirmation either, it should be pursued until we feel at peace. It is not negotiation—it is spiritual umpiring.

Word Definitions: **peace between individuals:** i.e., harmony, concord, security, safety, prosperity, felicity, (because peace and harmony make and keep things safe and prosperous)
rule: umpire, decide
thankful: mindful of favors, grateful
richly: abundantly
teaching: to hold discourse with others in order to instruct

What do these verses tell us about how we apply wisdom? What does this look like in our everyday lives?

Read Colossians 4:2-6:

Further Instructions
2 Continue steadfastly in prayer, being watchful in it with thanksgiving. 3 At the same time, pray also for us, that God may open to us a door for the word, to declare the mystery of Christ, on account of which I am in prison— 4 that I may make it clear, which is how I ought to speak.

5 Walk in wisdom toward outsiders, making the best use of the time. 6 Let your speech always be gracious, seasoned with salt, so that you may know how you ought to answer each person.

_____
_____
_____
_____
_____

LESSON 3:
HOW DO WE RECEIVE THIS WISDOM?

As we are seeking wisdom, we are to stay in earnest prayer, with thanksgiving that God would open doors for us. We don't need to force things open. We don't need to go make things happen. We need wisdom. We need to know how to act, how to proceed, what to do next. God is to open up the doors. We are not to go do it ourselves and cause all kinds of trouble. If we have issues, if we are dealing with outsiders, if we are dealing with people who might be opposing us, if we are dealing with opposition, we are to pray that God opens up the doors. Our role is to be graceful, respectful, and know exactly what to say and when to say it as God opens up the doors. He will give us wisdom so we don't get sucked into something that we shouldn't be sucked into and end up wasting our time, losing our peace, and causing us to have all kinds of trouble because we didn't even ask Him.

Trust Him to lead and guide us as we are following. He will open up doors and show us what and when to speak; this is His wisdom. It is His to give and ours to receive and follow.

Word Definitions: **manifest:** make the invisible, the truth, clear and visible
walk: to make one's way, progress; to make due, use of opportunities
redeem: to make wise and sacred use of every opportunity for doing good
grace: that which affords joy, pleasure, delight, sweetness, charm, loveliness: grace of speech; good will, loving-kindness, favor
salt: taste and preservation

Write in journal: What is God inviting you to consider in strengthening your ability to receive wisdom from Him? Go back over your list of questions/unresolved issues for which you seek wisdom (from introductory exercise) and pray together for wisdom from God.

LESSON 4:
EXPERIENCING THE FULLNESS OF WISDOM—THE SUPERNATURAL

6. **Experiencing the Supernatural (Power; Prophetic; Miraculous).**

As God gives us wisdom, what should we expect? What does this mean to us personally?

> **Read 1 Corinthians 2:1-5:**
>
> Proclaiming Christ Crucified
> **2** And I, when I came to you, brothers,[a] did not come proclaiming to you the testimony[b] of God with lofty speech or wisdom. ² For I decided to know nothing among you except Jesus Christ and him crucified. ³ And I was with you in weakness and in fear and much trembling, ⁴ and my speech and my message were not in plausible words of wisdom, but in demonstration of the Spirit and of power, ⁵ so that your faith might not rest in the wisdom of men[c] but in the power of God.

> "Wisdom is getting us in the right place at the right time with the right people so that He can fulfill His power."

_____
_____
_____
_____
_____

God says that as we receive His wisdom, we will experience His power along with it. This is the manifestation of His supernatural work. His wisdom comes with the demonstration of God doing all that His wisdom is. It's God fulfilling and bearing witness to what He wants to do. Wisdom is getting us in the right place at the right time with the right people so that He can fulfill His power. Wow. Wisdom means that we can change circumstances once He is able to get us to the right place. And that's why the pathway of God is so important for us to follow, so that He can deliver goodness to us. It's not us maneuvering through this difficult life, it's where God can deliver His power in our difficult lives.

LESSON 4:
EXPERIENCING THE FULLNESS OF WISDOM—THE SUPERNATURAL

Word Definitions: **demonstration:** manifest, made real, proved out real
power: external force, mighty, might, to do, mighty authority

What does God say about Him bearing witness to such a great salvation that we are to experience? Why? What can we then expect in our lives?

> **Read Hebrews 2:1-4**
>
> Warning Against Neglecting Salvation
> **2** Therefore we must pay much closer attention to what we have heard, lest we drift away from it. ² For since the message declared by angels proved to be reliable, and every transgression or disobedience received a just retribution,³ how shall we escape if we neglect such a great salvation? It was declared at first by the Lord, and it was attested to us by those who heard, ⁴ while God also bore witness by signs and wonders and various miracles and by gifts of the Holy Spirit distributed according to his will.

_____
_____
_____
_____
_____

God will prove out His will as we seek and declare His will (not neglecting so great a salvation) by bearing witness with miracles, miracles, miracles and the gifts of the Holy Spirit. He is going to work though us with the manifestation of the gifts of the Holy Spirit. Let's look at that next.

Word Definitions: **neglect:** careless, negligent
honor: dignity, riches, abundance
wonders: miracles
miracles: same word as power (dunamis)
gifts: distributions to us

LESSON 4:
EXPERIENCING THE FULLNESS OF WISDOM—THE SUPERNATURAL

What are these gifts of the Holy Spirit? How are they manifested through us, and what does that mean in our lives?

> **Read 1 Corinthians 12:1-11:**
>
> Spiritual Gifts
> **12** Now concerning[a] spiritual gifts,[b] brothers,[c] I do not want you to be uninformed. ² You know that when you were pagans you were led astray to mute idols, however you were led. ³ Therefore I want you to understand that no one speaking in the Spirit of God ever says "Jesus is accursed!" and no one can say "Jesus is Lord" except in the Holy Spirit.
>
> ⁴ Now there are varieties of gifts, but the same Spirit; ⁵ and there are varieties of service, but the same Lord; ⁶ and there are varieties of activities, but it is the same God who empowers them all in everyone. ⁷ To each is given the manifestation of the Spirit for the common good. ⁸ For to one is given through the Spirit the utterance of wisdom, and to another the utterance of knowledge according to the same Spirit, ⁹ to another faith by the same Spirit, to another gifts of healing by the one Spirit, ¹⁰ to another the working of miracles, to another prophecy, to another the ability to distinguish between spirits, to another various kinds of tongues, to another the interpretation of tongues. ¹¹ All these are empowered by one and the same Spirit, who apportions to each one individually as he wills.

_____
_____
_____
_____
_____

    We have the Holy Spirit resident within us, and as was said in Hebrews 2:4, God is going to manifest the gifts of the Holy Spirit through us in a variety of ways and in a variety of situations. It's going to be done in our lives, and He gives a whole litany of these.

    God is going to speak a word of knowledge, something that He knows about somebody's life. It might be something that happened in the past, and we are to speak to what God has shown us. How did we know that? God gave us a word of knowledge. God also uses faith, healing, miracles, and prophecy.

LESSON 4:
EXPERIENCING THE FULLNESS OF WISDOM—THE SUPERNATURAL

Prophecy can be either foretelling, something that is going to occur in the future, or forthtelling, which is truth being brought into our life right now. Discernment. Tongues and interpretation of tongues.

All of these things are our manifestation of the Spirit, which are miraculously happening when? At a specific moment, when needed. Who are we bringing this for? The body of Christ for the edification of God's people, for His glory. It's always in a situation, in a moment, where we're exercising this gift of the Spirit for somebody else in the body of Christ. We do not permanently have this gift. People get this confused. Some may have the gift of wisdom and others don't. Those who don't have the gift of wisdom might seek out those who do, but this is not what we are called to do. If we lack wisdom, what are we to do? Ask Him. God will give wisdom to us. He does not instruct us to go to someone else and get it. People are not given a permanent gift of wisdom, which is why we should always seek God for wisdom. Without faith it is impossible to please Him so we all must have faith. There is not only one individual with that gift and that's all he has.

God is saying that the manifestation of the gifts of the Spirit are such special moments for the body of Christ that there'll be a spectacular, supernatural giving of gifts to us. It will be manifested in an unusual way for the building up of the body. And God says, "I'm giving that through you, and next week it can be through somebody else." It could be a prophetic word that somebody gives to say that they hear God saying this, which, by the way, is always encouraging, comforting, and instructive. He says that this is going to happen all the time. Which implies that we're in community and we're exercising those gifts on behalf of somebody else. Expect it, enjoy it, and exercise these gifts as so directed by God.

Word Definitions:

manifests: make actual and visible, realized, to make known by teaching to become manifest, of a person

word: uttered by a living voice, embodies a conception or idea, what someone has said, the sayings of God

wisdom: the act of interpreting dreams and always giving the sagest advice, the intelligence evinced in discovering the meaning of some mysterious number or vision, skill in the management of affairs, devout and proper prudence in discourse with men

knowledge: knowledge signifies in general intelligence, understanding, to learn to know, come to know, get a knowledge of, perceive, feel

faith: conviction of the truth of anything, belief; in the New Testament: of a conviction or belief respecting man's relationship to God and divine things, generally with the included idea of trust and holy fervor born of faith and joined with it

healing: to cure, heal, to make whole, to free from errors and sins, to bring about (one's) salvation

LESSON 4:
EXPERIENCING THE FULLNESS OF WISDOM—THE SUPERNATURAL

miracles: strength power, ability, inherent power, power residing in a thing by virtue of its nature, or which a person or thing exerts and puts forth, power for performing miracles

prophecy: a discourse emanating from divine inspiration and declaring the purposes of God, whether by reproving and admonishing the wicked, or comforting the afflicted, or revealing things hidden; especially by foretelling future events

discernment: to separate, make a distinction, discriminate, to prefer, to learn by discrimination, to try, decide, to determine, give judgment, decide a dispute

tongue: the language or dialect used by a particular people distinct from that of other nations

interpretation: to translate what has been spoken or written in a foreign tongue into the vernacular

7.   **How do we Experience this Supernatural Work in our real lives with "Christ in us?"**

As we read these stories, what are the keys to experiencing the supernatural work of God as we walk in wisdom? How will these be experienced by us in our lives?

> **Read Matthew 8:1-13; 23-27:**
>
> Jesus Cleanses a Leper
> **8** When he came down from the mountain, great crowds followed him. ² And behold, a leper[a] came to him and knelt before him, saying, "Lord, if you will, you can make me clean." ³ And Jesus[b] stretched out his hand and touched him, saying, "I will; be clean." And immediately his leprosy was cleansed. ⁴ And Jesus said to him, "See that you say nothing to anyone, but go, show yourself to the priest and offer the gift that Moses commanded, for a proof to them."
>
> The Faith of a Centurion
> ⁵ When he had entered Capernaum, a centurion came forward to him, appealing to him, ⁶ "Lord, my servant is lying paralyzed at home, suffering terribly." ⁷ And he said to him, "I will come and heal him." ⁸ But the centurion replied, "Lord, I am not worthy to have you come under my roof, but only say the word, and my servant will be healed. ⁹ For I too am a man under authority, with soldiers under me. And I say to one, 'Go,' and he goes, and to another, 'Come,' and he comes, and to

LESSON 4:
EXPERIENCING THE FULLNESS OF WISDOM—THE SUPERNATURAL

> my servant,[c] 'Do this,' and he does it." [10] When Jesus heard this, he marveled and said to those who followed him, "Truly, I tell you, with no one in Israel[d] have I found such faith. [11] I tell you, many will come from east and west and recline at table with Abraham, Isaac, and Jacob in the kingdom of heaven,[12] while the sons of the kingdom will be thrown into the outer darkness. In that place there will be weeping and gnashing of teeth." [13] And to the centurion Jesus said, "Go; let it be done for you as you have believed." And the servant was healed at that very moment.
>
> **Jesus Calms a Storm**
> [23] And when he got into the boat, his disciples followed him. [24] And behold, there arose a great storm on the sea, so that the boat was being swamped by the waves; but he was asleep. [25] And they went and woke him, saying, "Save us, Lord; we are perishing." [26] And he said to them, "Why are you afraid, O you of little faith?" Then he rose and rebuked the winds and the sea, and there was a great calm. [27] And the men marveled, saying, "What sort of man is this, that even winds and sea obey him?"

_____
_____
_____
_____
_____

The leper came to Jesus and asked a simple question: "Are You willing to help me?" Jesus said He was. Here it is. And the leper experienced the supernatural because there is a willingness by God to perform exactly what we ask for—so ask.

The centurion had a servant who was lying paralyzed and suffering terribly; he asked Jesus if He would come heal his servant? Jesus said yes. The centurion then said, You do not actually have to come – just speak Your Word; as he understood authority and healing. He knew the supernatural comes from Jesus speaking His spiritual Word, which has authority over material things.

As we seek wisdom from God, ask: "What do You have to say about this particular issue? It's not only about what You want us to do, rather, the primary questions are, 'What are You going to do? What do You speak about this? What's Your promise about that?'" And once we know, then we can pray that and start seeing God's miraculous work because we can now understand that this is about His authority, it's His supernatural work that can occur.

LESSON 4:
EXPERIENCING THE FULLNESS OF WISDOM—THE SUPERNATURAL

Later, the disciples had a problem. There was a storm, a strong circumstance against them. Jesus asked them if they understood that if they were to believe, they could not only handle the storm but they then would have access to the power to overcome it?

He is giving us the wisdom to expand our view of the spiritual life available to us. Not to just tell us how to get out of the storm. Rather, that we, through faith (receiving what He says, what He speaks), have the authority, the power to speak to this storm, this circumstance, and have it overcome. These stories show us the amazing power that, through wisdom, we have in our lives to resolve our issues—not just asking God what we are to do—rather, asking, "What are You going to do?"

Word Definitions:

touch: to fasten one's self to, adhere to, cling to
summon: to call to one's side, call for, summon
heal: cure, restore to health
speak: command
word: logos
authority: the power of rule or government (the power of him whose will and commands must be submitted to by others and obeyed)
faith: conviction of the truth of anything
believed: to think to be true, to be persuaded of, to credit, place confidence in
done: come to pass, happen
sick: miserable, ill
took: to take in order to carry away
infirmities: feebleness of health or sickness of the soul
bore: to take up in order to carry or bear, to put upon one's self (something) to be carried
sickness: disease
tempest: great shaking, like earthquake
little faith: trusting too little
rebuked: commanded, charge sharply
obey: submit to

LESSON 4:
EXPERIENCING THE FULLNESS OF WISDOM—THE SUPERNATURAL

What do we learn from these two stories about how God's supernatural power is manifested in our lives? How do we apply this to our lives?

Read Matthew 9:18-31:

A Girl Restored to Life and a Woman Healed
18 While he was saying these things to them, behold, a ruler came in and knelt before him, saying, "My daughter has just died, but come and lay your hand on her, and she will live." 19 And Jesus rose and followed him, with his disciples. 20 And behold, a woman who had suffered from a discharge of blood for twelve years came up behind him and touched the fringe of his garment, 21 for she said to herself, "If I only touch his garment, I will be made well." 22 Jesus turned, and seeing her he said, "Take heart, daughter; your faith has made you well." And instantly[a] the woman was made well. 23 And when Jesus came to the ruler's house and saw the flute players and the crowd making a commotion, 24 he said, "Go away, for the girl is not dead but sleeping." And they laughed at him. 25 But when the crowd had been put outside, he went in and took her by the hand, and the girl arose. 26 And the report of this went through all that district.

Jesus Heals Two Blind Men
27 And as Jesus passed on from there, two blind men followed him, crying aloud, "Have mercy on us, Son of David." 28 When he entered the house, the blind men came to him, and Jesus said to them, "Do you believe that I am able to do this?" They said to him, "Yes, Lord." 29 Then he touched their eyes, saying, "According to your faith be it done to you." 30 And their eyes were opened. And Jesus sternly warned them, "See that no one knows about it." 31 But they went away and spread his fame through all that district.

_____
_____
_____
_____
_____

LESSON 4:
EXPERIENCING THE FULLNESS OF WISDOM—THE SUPERNATURAL

In the first story, a woman with bleeding for 12 years says: "If I can just get to touch the hem of His garment, I can be healed." And she winds up getting through the crowd, going after it, going after it, going after it until she touches it. And she's healed. Of course, Jesus says, "Who touched Me? Power's gone out of Me." And He says to her, "Be of good cheer, your faith has made you well."

If we believe something that's absolutely true, we will be healed. What exactly did she believe? Let's look at this deeper.

Word Definitions: **touch:** to fasten one's self to, adhere to, cling to
hem: in the New Testament, a little appendage hanging down from the edge of the mantle or cloak, made of twisted wool, a tassel, tuft: the Jews had such appendages attached to their mantles to remind them of the law
whole: (sozo – heal): to save, keep safe and sound, to rescue one from danger or destruction (from injury or peril), to save a suffering one (from perishing), i.e., one suffering from disease, to make well, heal, restore to health

What does this reveal to us about the truth of the Hem of His Garment? What does this mean spiritually to us?

Read Numbers 15:37-41:

Tassels on Garments
[37] The Lord said to Moses, [38] "Speak to the people of Israel, and tell them to make tassels on the corners of their garments throughout their generations, and to put a cord of blue on the tassel of each corner. [39] And it shall be a tassel for you to look at and remember all the commandments of the Lord, to do them, not to follow[a] after your own heart and your own eyes, which you are inclined to whore after. [40] So you shall remember and do all my commandments, and be holy to your God. [41] I am the Lord your God, who brought you out of the land of Egypt to be your God: I am the Lord your God."

_____
_____
_____
_____
_____

LESSON 4:
EXPERIENCING THE FULLNESS OF WISDOM—THE SUPERNATURAL

In the hem of His garment is this blue line, this thread. There are tassels there to have us remember all that God has done for us and all the commandments He gave for us to surrender our will to His. The tassels are a symbol that we are to follow Him with all our heart, not to seek our own way, or make our own decisions, but instead to always seek His wisdom. He reminds us to keep following Him, keep following Him, keep following Him. Surrender our will to Him, and it will go well for us.

Word Definitions: **fringe:** tassel, lock
remember: recall, call to mind, to be brought to remembrance
commandments: charge, give orders, lay charge, give charge to, order

What do these verses say are resident in His wings (Hem of His garment)? What does this then mean about healing and pursuing the Hem of His garment?

> **Read Malachi 4:2-3:**
>
> ² But for you who fear my name, the sun of righteousness shall rise with healing in its wings. You shall go out leaping like calves from the stall. ³ And you shall tread down the wicked, for they will be ashes under the soles of your feet, on the day when I act, says the Lord of hosts.

_____
_____
_____
_____
_____

Christ (righteousness) is going to come with healing in His wings. The Hebrew words noted are "healing in the hem of His garment." The power of healing is in Him, in this hem of His garment, which reminds us that we are to remember all that "I am," to surrender our will to Him, to follow Him completely, to believe in His truth and His life. These will bring health and healing.

LESSON 4:
EXPERIENCING THE FULLNESS OF WISDOM—THE SUPERNATURAL

Word Definitions: **healing:** make healthful, to heal, of God, healer, of hurts of nations involving restored favor, of individual distresses
wing: extremity, edge, winged, border, corner, extremity, skirt, corner (of garment)

As above, what do these verses say are resident in His wings (Hem of His garment)? What does this then mean about healing and pursuing the Hem of His garment?

> **Read Psalm 36:5-12:**
>
> 5 Your steadfast love, O Lord, extends to the heavens,
>   your faithfulness to the clouds.
> 6 Your righteousness is like the mountains of God;
>   your judgments are like the great deep;
>   man and beast you save, O Lord.
> 7 How precious is your steadfast love, O God!
>   The children of mankind take refuge in the shadow of your wings.
> 8 They feast on the abundance of your house,
>   and you give them drink from the river of your delights.
> 9 For with you is the fountain of life;
>   in your light do we see light.
> 10 Oh, continue your steadfast love to those who know you,
>   and your righteousness to the upright of heart!
> 11 Let not the foot of arrogance come upon me,
>   nor the hand of the wicked drive me away.
> 12 There the evildoers lie fallen;
>   they are thrust down, unable to rise.

_____
_____
_____
_____
_____

This phrase, "steadfast love" in Hebrew is "covenant loyalty," which means He's going to bless us to make us a blessing in the shadow of Christ's wing. And again, the Hebrew is in the "hem of His garment"—the place of the covenant—the pleasures of life, the abundance of life. Everything is available in the hem of His garment.

LESSON 4:
EXPERIENCING THE FULLNESS OF WISDOM—THE SUPERNATURAL

The woman with the issue of blood put two and two together. She was a follower of the truth of the Old Testament, and there was one thing that she knew for certain, and that was that she was willing to surrender her will and follow Him. He is the Messiah, the embodiment of all of this. The abundant life is Him, His life. It's healing. It's in the hem of His garment. Now, it wasn't a mystical, magical thing. It was Him. And if she could just touch that hem, the power would be there, and she would be healed. She was going to be healed. She believed that. She makes her way to it and touches it and is immediately healed. There were no conversations. She simply got to it.

And Jesus says, "Who touched me? Power has gone out from me. Your faith has healed you, you believed. You put the whole thing together. You grabbed it."

He continued, "It was your faith, your belief. Your spiritual understanding to receive supernatural power; you got to the right time, at the right place; you received it because supernatural work happened because you fulfilled wisdom." That's what it's all about. Are we following what He's saying to get to the right time, at the right place, with the right people, and drawing the power of what He's to speak to us? But, of course, it's more about what He will speak and do than just what we are able to do in any situation.

Word Definitions: **wing:** extremity, edge, winged, border, corner, skirt, corner (of garment)
pleasures: luxury, dainty, delight, finery
fountain: spring, of source of life, joy, purification
life: revival, renewal
light: to shine; to become bright, to be illuminated

What do these verses say about our experiencing God's supernatural work in our lives?

Read Acts 1:5-8:

5 for John baptized with water, but you will be baptized with[a] the Holy Spirit not many days from now."

The Ascension
6 So when they had come together, they asked him, "Lord, will you at this time restore the kingdom to Israel?" 7 He said to them, "It is not for you to know times or seasons that the Father has fixed by his own authority. 8 But you will receive power when the Holy Spirit has come upon you, and you will be my witnesses in Jerusalem and in all Judea and Samaria, and to the end of the earth."

LESSON 4:
EXPERIENCING THE FULLNESS OF WISDOM—THE SUPERNATURAL

_____
_____
_____
_____
_____

As we walk in the Spirit, receiving His wisdom, we will be His witnesses to His power and to the miraculous. We'll perform miracles and be His witness. This will happen as He so directs us with wisdom to the places He intends, to the paths He wants us on, and it will be with power. We'll manifest the power He's going to give us to be His witnesses. With this power, He will be telling us what to say, when to say it, where to be, and with the power to deliver it so that His miraculous power manifests itself as we are His witnesses.

Word Definitions: **power:** splendor, majesty, beauty, vigor, glory, in-charge, control, have jurisdiction, power to influence, cause to become great; much; many; enlarged, exceedingly abundant, power (physical and spiritual) of doing supernatural, right to govern, rule, command - possessing authority, mighty work, strength, miracle, performing miracles, excellence

witness: in a legal sense

What happened at Pentecost that demonstrated His power of being a witness? How will this work on our lives?

> **Read Acts 2:1-4; 22:**
>
> The Coming of the Holy Spirit
> **2** When the day of Pentecost arrived, they were all together in one place. ² And suddenly there came from heaven a sound like a mighty rushing wind, and it filled the entire house where they were sitting. ³ And divided tongues as of fire appeared to them and rested[a] on each one of them. ⁴ And they were all filled with the Holy Spirit and began to speak in other tongues as the Spirit gave them utterance.
>
> ²² "Men of Israel, hear these words: Jesus of Nazareth, a man attested to you by God with mighty works and wonders and signs that God did through him in your midst, as you yourselves know—

LESSON 4:
EXPERIENCING THE FULLNESS OF WISDOM—THE SUPERNATURAL

_____
_____
_____
_____
_____

The Holy Spirit came upon them. They were of one accord. They started speaking in languages of all the people from different countries so that they could understand what was being spoken by one person, speaking his native language. And Peter says: "As I try to explain it to you, the reason I can talk to you about Jesus is because you all can attest to what? What Jesus did—miracles, signs, wonders, more miracles."

Peter also said: "You can have that life—not just a philosophy or a theology, or a religion of what people could learn about Jesus—but the supernatural, miraculous life of Jesus that was real to all of us. Three thousand people said, I want that. And we can see what happened next."

Word Definitions: **with one accord:** with one mind, with one passion
tongue: the language or dialect used by a particular people distinct from that of other nations
miracles: dunamis (same word as power)
wonders: real supernatural occurrences
signs: miracles and wonders of God

What happened for all the people who said yes to Peter and began to gather and receive the life, the wisdom of Christ? How does this apply to us?

> **Read Acts 2:40-47:**
>
> 40 And with many other words he bore witness and continued to exhort them, saying, "Save yourselves from this crooked generation." 41 So those who received his word were baptized, and there were added that day about three thousand souls.
>
> The Fellowship of the Believers
> 42 And they devoted themselves to the apostles' teaching and the fellowship, to the breaking of bread and the prayers. 43 And awe[a] came upon every soul, and many wonders and signs were being done through the apostles. 44 And all

LESSON 4:
EXPERIENCING THE FULLNESS OF WISDOM—THE SUPERNATURAL

> who believed were together and had all things in common. [45] And they were selling their possessions and belongings and distributing the proceeds to all, as any had need. [46] And day by day, attending the temple together and breaking bread in their homes, they received their food with glad and generous hearts, [47] praising God and having favor with all the people. And the Lord added to their number day by day those who were being saved.

_____
_____
_____
_____
_____

They started gathering together in house churches, basically, and listening to the truth of what Jesus had spoken to the disciples. They started sharing that, and they broke bread together during communion. They were praying. And remember, a prayer wasn't simply, "Isn't this a good idea?" Instead, they sought actual wisdom over their problems, or questions, or issues. They asked what God had to say about it and what His will was.

As they began learning what God says about how to hear His voice and receive wisdom about how to handle things, people were being encouraged and excited to keep growing in Christ because of the signs and wonders. They were in awe of all miraculous things that God was doing as He was giving them wisdom. And because of it, they said: "I want that. I want to experience that because real life stuff was happening." It wasn't philosophical. It was life experience of signs and wonders. They needed wisdom and lived out the wisdom that God was revealing and the power that came with it.

These people were living in a tough time. There was Roman oppression and Jewish oppression. But signs and wonders were happening in their lives all the time, which is why the church was exploding in growth. People heard about it and wanted this to happen for them.

Word Definitions:
- **continued steadfastly:** to adhere to one, be his adherent, to be devoted
- **wonders:** real supernatural occurrences
- **signs:** miracles and wonders by which God authenticates
- **gladness:** extreme joy
- **favor:** that which affords joy, pleasure, delight, sweetness, charm, loveliness: grace of speech, good will, loving-kindness

LESSON 4:
EXPERIENCING THE FULLNESS OF WISDOM—THE SUPERNATURAL

How did Peter and John demonstrate the supernatural work of God as they were living out God's wisdom? How does this apply to us?

> **Read Acts 3:1-10; 16:**
>
> The Lame Beggar Healed
>
> **3** Now Peter and John were going up to the temple at the hour of prayer, the ninth hour.[a] **2** And a man lame from birth was being carried, whom they laid daily at the gate of the temple that is called the Beautiful Gate to ask alms of those entering the temple. **3** Seeing Peter and John about to go into the temple, he asked to receive alms. **4** And Peter directed his gaze at him, as did John, and said, "Look at us." **5** And he fixed his attention on them, expecting to receive something from them. **6** But Peter said, "I have no silver and gold, but what I do have I give to you. In the name of Jesus Christ of Nazareth, rise up and walk!" **7** And he took him by the right hand and raised him up, and immediately his feet and ankles were made strong. **8** And leaping up, he stood and began to walk, and entered the temple with them, walking and leaping and praising God. **9** And all the people saw him walking and praising God, **10** and recognized him as the one who sat at the Beautiful Gate of the temple, asking for alms. And they were filled with wonder and amazement at what had happened to him. **16** And his name—by faith in his name—has made this man strong whom you see and know, and the faith that is through Jesus[a] has given the man this perfect health in the presence of you all.

_____
_____
_____
_____
_____

As Peter and John were going to the temple, a man who was disabled was seeking money to live on; he was begging. They had real wisdom: They did not give him money, but instead gave him what they truly had, which was the authority to bring healing. Then Peter tells us that this is not him or his skill but that it is faith. Faith in the power, the authority of the name of Christ. The wisdom that He has is available is to give us the supernatural power of healing, which is going to change our whole life. Wisdom expands our understanding of the supernatural and how we can exercise it.

LESSON 4:
EXPERIENCING THE FULLNESS OF WISDOM—THE SUPERNATURAL

Word Definitions: **look:** see, discern

have: own, have in my possession, possess

strength: make firm, solid

name: i.e., for one's rank, authority, interests, pleasure, command, excellences, deeds, etc.

faith: conviction of the truth of anything

give: bestow a gift, to grant, give to one asking, let have, to supply, furnish necessary things, to give over, deliver

soundness: complete in all its parts, in no part wanting or unsound, complete, entire, whole

In this story, how does God work in the lives of both Saul and Ananias? What does this teach us about wisdom and how we apply this in our lives?

> **Read Acts 9:1-19:**
>
> The Conversion of Saul
> **9** But Saul, still breathing threats and murder against the disciples of the Lord, went to the high priest [2] and asked him for letters to the synagogues at Damascus, so that if he found any belonging to the Way, men or women, he might bring them bound to Jerusalem. [3] Now as he went on his way, he approached Damascus, and suddenly a light from heaven shone around him. [4] And falling to the ground, he heard a voice saying to him, "Saul, Saul, why are you persecuting me?" [5] And he said, "Who are you, Lord?" And he said, "I am Jesus, whom you are persecuting. 6 But rise and enter the city, and you will be told what you are to do." [7] The men who were traveling with him stood speechless, hearing the voice but seeing no one. [8] Saul rose from the ground, and although his eyes were opened, he saw nothing. So they led him by the hand and brought him into Damascus. [9] And for three days he was without sight, and neither ate nor drank.
>
> [10] Now there was a disciple at Damascus named Ananias. The Lord said to him in a vision, "Ananias." And he said, "Here I am, Lord." [11] And the Lord said to him, "Rise and go to the street called Straight, and at the house of Judas look for a man of Tarsus named Saul, for behold, he is praying, [12] and he has seen in a vision a man named Ananias come in and lay his hands on him so that he might regain his sight." [13] But Ananias answered, "Lord, I have heard from many about this man, how much evil he has done to your saints at Jerusalem. [14] And here

LESSON 4:
EXPERIENCING THE FULLNESS OF WISDOM—THE SUPERNATURAL

> he has authority from the chief priests to bind all who call on your name." [15] But the Lord said to him, "Go, for he is a chosen instrument of mine to carry my name before the Gentiles and kings and the children of Israel. [16] For I will show him how much he must suffer for the sake of my name." [17] So Ananias departed and entered the house. And laying his hands on him he said, "Brother Saul, the Lord Jesus who appeared to you on the road by which you came has sent me so that you may regain your sight and be filled with the Holy Spirit." [18] And immediately something like scales fell from his eyes, and he regained his sight. Then he rose and was baptized; [19] and taking food, he was strengthened.
>
> Saul Proclaims Jesus in Synagogues
> For some days he was with the disciples at Damascus.

_____
_____
_____
_____
_____

Christ meets Saul on the road to Damascus and causes him to lose his sight. Saul asks Christ,

"What do you want me to do?" He is told to go into the city and wait and he loses the sight.

Then God speaks to Ananias, who's a disciple, a follower of God, and is used to hearing His voice. God tells him to go into the city to a specific address and go lay hands on Saul. He responds by saying: "Do You know who You are talking about? This does not make sense. He'll probably put me in jail so, no, I really do not wish to go do this. It just does not make sense to me." God says: "I understand, but I'm telling you that he is converted, he is now a believer." It's interesting to note that God tells Ananias something that nobody else has ever heard before. Saul (Paul) will be taking the message of the gospel to the Gentiles. So, Ananias goes, and Saul receives the Spirit and begins his walk with God.

As we are seeking wisdom, we often struggle with instructions that do not make sense, or are difficult to follow. God says: "It's okay if you don't understand. Stay with Me and seek more insight, more information. Let Me give you some more detail."

LESSON 4:
EXPERIENCING THE FULLNESS OF WISDOM—THE SUPERNATURAL

God is always working both sides of the process, which is why we can trust that our part is to follow His wisdom, even when it does not make perfect sense to us.

Word Definition: **vision:** a sight divinely granted

How did God work both sides of this story and give wisdom to fulfill His bigger story? Why is this so important in our seeking wisdom and following Him?

> **Read Acts 10:8-38:**
>
> 8 and having related everything to them, he sent them to Joppa.
>
> Peter's Vision
> 9 The next day, as they were on their journey and approaching the city, Peter went up on the housetop about the sixth hour[a] to pray. 10 And he became hungry and wanted something to eat, but while they were preparing it, he fell into a trance 11 and saw the heavens opened and something like a great sheet descending, being let down by its four corners upon the earth. 12 In it were all kinds of animals and reptiles and birds of the air. 13 And there came a voice to him: "Rise, Peter; kill and eat." 14 But Peter said, "By no means, Lord; for I have never eaten anything that is common or unclean." 15 And the voice came to him again a second time, "What God has made clean, do not call common." 16 This happened three times, and the thing was taken up at once to heaven.
>
> 17 Now while Peter was inwardly perplexed as to what the vision that he had seen might mean, behold, the men who were sent by Cornelius, having made inquiry for Simon's house, stood at the gate 18 and called out to ask whether Simon who was called Peter was lodging there. 19 And while Peter was pondering the vision, the Spirit said to him, "Behold, three men are looking for you. 20 Rise and go down and accompany them without hesitation,[b] for I have sent them." 21 And Peter went down to the men and said, "I am the one you are looking for. What is the reason for your coming?" 22 And they said, "Cornelius, a centurion, an upright and God-fearing man, who is well spoken of by the whole Jewish nation, was directed by a holy angel to send for you to come to his house and to hear what you have to say." 23 So he invited them in to be his guests.

LESSON 4:
EXPERIENCING THE FULLNESS OF WISDOM—THE SUPERNATURAL

The next day he rose and went away with them, and some of the brothers from Joppa accompanied him. 24 And on the following day they entered Caesarea. Cornelius was expecting them and had called together his relatives and close friends. 25 When Peter entered, Cornelius met him and fell down at his feet and worshiped him. 26 But Peter lifted him up, saying, "Stand up; I too am a man." 27 And as he talked with him, he went in and found many persons gathered. 28 And he said to them, "You yourselves know how unlawful it is for a Jew to associate with or to visit anyone of another nation, but God has shown me that I should not call any person common or unclean. 29 So when I was sent for, I came without objection. I ask then why you sent for me."

30 And Cornelius said, "Four days ago, about this hour, I was praying in my house at the ninth hour,[c] and behold, a man stood before me in bright clothing 31 and said, 'Cornelius, your prayer has been heard and your alms have been remembered before God. 32 Send therefore to Joppa and ask for Simon who is called Peter. He is lodging in the house of Simon, a tanner, by the sea.' 33 So I sent for you at once, and you have been kind enough to come. Now therefore we are all here in the presence of God to hear all that you have been commanded by the Lord."

Gentiles Hear the Good News
34 So Peter opened his mouth and said: "Truly I understand that God shows no partiality, 35 but in every nation anyone who fears him and does what is right is acceptable to him. 36 As for the word that he sent to Israel, preaching good news of peace through Jesus Christ (he is Lord of all), 37 you yourselves know what happened throughout all Judea, beginning from Galilee after the baptism that John proclaimed: 38 how God anointed Jesus of Nazareth with the Holy Spirit and with power. He went about doing good and healing all who were oppressed by the devil, for God was with him.

_____
_____
_____
_____
_____

LESSON 4:
EXPERIENCING THE FULLNESS OF WISDOM—THE SUPERNATURAL

Cornelius is seeking to know God, so an angel appears to him and says for him to send for Peter and have Peter explain things to him.

Peter receives a new vision that is completely against his paradigm so he says, "No, I cannot follow what You have instructed me to do in this vision." So, he's pondering, wondering what this is all about. While he is processing all this, Cornelius' soldiers come to Peter's house and the Holy Spirit tells Peter to go with them. That was an instruction that Peter could easily accept because he's heard that before so was comfortable with it. As he was going, he continues processing, "God, what is all this about? I'm walking with Gentiles being sent by the Holy Spirit, You gave me a vision of everything, don't call anything unclean. Are you telling me this is about the Gentiles?" He's pondering, discussing, pondering, discussing, watching, listening, watching, waiting. At Cornelius' house, where Cornelius has brought his whole family and lots of friends to hear what Peter has to say, it all becomes clear to Peter.

And Peter says: "I understand. I perceive there is no partiality with God. The gospel is for everybody, not just the Jews. Wow! This is an amazing truth, and I now understand."

The people wanted to be baptized. They were so overwhelmed by the Holy Spirit, they began to speak in tongues. And all the Jews around Peter saw the whole thing, too. This was the beginning of the Gentile ministry.

It took a pursuit of wisdom, although it was a complete struggle. Our role is to keep pursuing it and let God continue to reveal pieces of the truth until it all comes together. God says that He will work both sides of things and will keep working in a way that we can understand. He will take this unbelievable thought and translate it into how we do understand it, which will be supernatural.

Word Definitions: **common:** ordinary
unclean: to the Jews by prohibition from Levitical law
doubted: to be entirely at loss, to be in perplexity
mean: what could be
sent: to order (one) to go to a place appointed
show: taught, revealed
hear: to understand, perceive the sense of what is said
commanded: ordered, appointed
perceive: to lay hold of to make one's own, to obtain, attain to, to take into one's self, appropriate
no respecter of persons: everyone same to God

LESSON 4:
EXPERIENCING THE FULLNESS OF WISDOM—THE SUPERNATURAL

What do these verses speak to how we play an important role in exercising God's supernatural work? What can we thus expect in our lives?

> **Read Luke 9:1-6; 10:17-20:**
>
> Jesus Sends Out the Twelve Apostles
> **9** And he called the twelve together and gave them power and authority over all demons and to cure diseases, ² and he sent them out to proclaim the kingdom of God and to heal. ³ And he said to them, "Take nothing for your journey, no staff, nor bag, nor bread, nor money; and do not have two tunics. [a] ⁴ And whatever house you enter, stay there, and from there depart. ⁵ And wherever they do not receive you, when you leave that town shake off the dust from your feet as a testimony against them." 6 And they departed and went through the villages, preaching the gospel and healing everywhere.
>
> The Return of the Seventy-Two
> ¹⁷ The seventy-two returned with joy, saying, "Lord, even the demons are subject to us in your name!" ¹⁸ And he said to them, "I saw Satan fall like lightning from heaven. ¹⁹ Behold, I have given you authority to tread on serpents and scorpions, and over all the power of the enemy, and nothing shall hurt you. ²⁰ Nevertheless, do not rejoice in this, that the spirits are subject to you, but rejoice that your names are written in heaven."

_____
_____
_____
_____

We're going to be exercising this authority of what He speaks, what He does, and what He's going to fulfill. And it's fulfilling the supernatural on our path. And this is why He needs to get us on the right path so that we can exercise it in our lives and see the great and mighty things that He's about ready to do.

Word Definitions: **give:** bestow, grant, deliver over
power: dunamis; authority
authority: rule, dominion
cure: heal

LESSON 4:
EXPERIENCING THE FULLNESS OF WISDOM—THE SUPERNATURAL

Word Definitions: **kingdom:** rule, authority, dominion
heal: make whole, restore
subject: obey, yield, submit to
all: each and every

What is the role of unity in experiencing the supernatural? How does this work in our everyday lives?

Read Matthew 18:18-20:

18 Truly, I say to you, whatever you bind on earth shall be bound in heaven, and whatever you loose on earth shall be loosed[a] in heaven. **19** Again I say to you, if two of you agree on earth about anything they ask, it will be done for them by my Father in heaven. **20** For where two or three are gathered in my name, there am I among them."

_____

_____

_____

_____

Read Psalm 133:

When Brothers Dwell in Unity
A Song of Ascents. Of David.

133 Behold, how good and pleasant it is
    when brothers dwell in unity![a]
2 It is like the precious oil on the head,
    running down on the beard,
on the beard of Aaron,
    running down on the collar of his robes!
3 It is like the dew of Hermon,
    which falls on the mountains of Zion!
For there the Lord has commanded the blessing,
    life forevermore.

LESSON 4:
EXPERIENCING THE FULLNESS OF WISDOM—THE SUPERNATURAL

_____
_____
_____
_____
_____

    We are to gather in His name, seek His wisdom, and ask for His will. We are to look for what He has to say. Come to an agreement together because unity will lead us to His will, and as Psalm 133 says, "There I will command blessing. Unity leads you to my will and that is where the power resides the power to bind and loose. You can come against the enemy, and you can loose the very power of heaven supernaturally into your situation. It's just not about what you do. It's about what you hear I want to do and come to an agreement on that. And that's where your prayer time would be." What are we hearing? We together can pray, and in faith, know that what we have heard will happen supernaturally.

    What's the wisdom of God for us to get on the right path at the right time with the right people for God to fulfill it?

Word Definitions: **agree:** come to unity, firm agreement without doubt
done: come to pass, happen
gathered together: joined together in unity
name: authority
pleasant: delightful, sweet, lovely, agreeable, beautiful
dwell: remain, sit, abide
unity: join, unite, be joined, be united
command: charge, give orders, lay charge, give charge to, order
blessings: prosperity

As we reach unity and understand authority in that unity, how are we to pray? What does that mean to us personally?

> **Read Mark 11:20-25:**
>
> The Lesson from the Withered Fig Tree
> [20] As they passed by in the morning, they saw the fig tree withered away to its roots. [21] And Peter remembered and said to him, "Rabbi, look! The fig tree that you cursed has withered." [22] And Jesus answered them, "Have faith in

LESSON 4:
EXPERIENCING THE FULLNESS OF WISDOM—THE SUPERNATURAL

> God.[23] Truly, I say to you, whoever says to this mountain, 'Be taken up and thrown into the sea,' and does not doubt in his heart, but believes that what he says will come to pass, it will be done for him. [24] Therefore I tell you, whatever you ask in prayer, believe that you have received[a] it, and it will be yours. [25] And whenever you stand praying, forgive, if you have anything against anyone, so that your Father also who is in heaven may forgive you your trespasses."[b]

_____
_____
_____
_____
_____

As we receive His word and we're praying what He says, believe we've already received it because that's what He sees, this is when the supernatural can happen. That's what our prayer life is all about. What do we hear God say? Speak it. See, it is already done, and it will happen. That's the process of wisdom. It isn't just what I do to maneuver through the problems, it's relying on God to resolve the problems. He's going to get us on the right path at the right time with the right people, with the right insight in the understanding so that we're following His instruction. Then we can fulfill His will, which is to command the covenant to bless us so that we can be a blessing. This is what wisdom is all about.

Word Definitions:

agree: come to unity, firm agreement without doubt
ask: don
doubt: waver, dispute about it
believe: think to be true
desire: ask, don
receive: take to one's self, to own, to possess
have: shall come about in reality

Write in journal: As you pray for wisdom for the questions or unresolved issues for which you seek wisdom, what are you hearing? What prophetic word is God giving you? What supernatural work of God is required to fulfill the answer to your question or issue?

www.ingramcontent.com/pod-product-compliance
Lightning Source LLC
Chambersburg PA
CBHW051258110526
44589CB00025B/2868